STORIES OF HOPE FROM AUSCHWITZ

STORIES OF HOPE FROM AUSCHWITZ

Copyright © Octopus Publishing Group Limited, 2026

All rights reserved.

Text by Peter Salmon

No part of this book may be reproduced by any means, nor transmitted, nor translated into a machine language, without the written permission of the publishers.

Condition of Sale
This book is sold subject to the condition that it shall not, by way of trade or otherwise, be lent, resold, hired out or otherwise circulated in any form of binding or cover other than that in which it is published and without a similar condition including this condition being imposed on the subsequent purchaser.

An Hachette UK Company
www.hachette.co.uk

Summersdale Publishers
Part of Octopus Publishing Group Limited
Carmelite House
50 Victoria Embankment
LONDON
EC4Y 0DZ
UK

This FSC® label means that materials and other controlled sources used for the product have been responsibly sourced

www.summersdale.com

The authorized representative in the EEA is Hachette Ireland, 8 Castlecourt Centre, Dublin 15, D15 XTP3, Ireland (email: info@hbgi.ie)

Printed and bound by Clays Ltd, Suffolk, NR35 1ED

ISBN: 978-1-83799-762-6
eISBN: 978-1-83799-763-3

Substantial discounts on bulk quantities of Summersdale books are available to corporations, professional associations and other organizations. For details contact general enquiries: telephone: +44 (0) 1243 771107 or email: enquiries@summersdale.com.

PETRA STEVENSON

STORIES OF HOPE FROM AUSCHWITZ

INSPIRING TRUE STORIES OF HOPE, LOVE AND SURVIVAL

DISCLAIMER

All the stories in this book have at some point been expressed in the public domain. Every effort has been made to ensure that all information is correct. The publisher apologizes for any errors or omissions and would be grateful if notified of any corrections that should be incorporated in future reprints or editions of this book.

INTRODUCTION

On 13 December 1943, a 24-year-old Italian chemist, Primo Levi, was captured by the militia while fighting for the resistance against Benito Mussolini's Fascist government. Mussolini had taken power in 1922, imposing a dictatorship. And in 1938, he had joined forces with the Chancellor of Germany – Adolf Hitler.

For all its brutality, Mussolini's Fascist state had not instituted any racial laws against its Jewish population. That changed in 1938 – a Manifesto of Race was circulated, stripping the Italian Jews of their citizenship, and dismissing them from all jobs. All relationships between Jews and other Italians were banned, and Jewish properties were confiscated. Primo Levi was Jewish.

He was initially interred at an Italian concentration camp in Fossoli, but, based on his surroundings and the attitude of those around him, there wasn't any indication of the horrors that were to come. "Our conditions in the camp were quite good. There was no talk of executions and the atmosphere was quite calm," he would later write in *If This Is a Man*. But Fossoli was just a holding station. On 21 February 1944, Levi and other Jewish prisoners-of-war were placed in 12 cramped cattle trucks and taken to their final destination, a concentration camp, 50 kilometres (31 miles) southwest of Kraków. Its name was Auschwitz.

What we know now, but what Levi, as the cattle truck passed through a gate with a sign reading *"Arbeit macht frei"* ("Work sets you free") above it, could not know, was that Auschwitz was a place where humanity plumbed the greatest depths of its capacity for cruelty and horror.

For the next 11 months, in conditions that resist description, he would suffer deprivations on an almost inhuman scale, including the murder of hundreds of those around him, who were herded into gas chambers and killed, their bodies then tipped into mass graves. Of the 650 Italian Jews who arrived in those cattle trucks, Levi was one of only 20 who left the camps alive.

When we talk about Auschwitz, it is easy to have our emotions paralyzed by the sheer numbers. It is estimated that 1.1 million men, women and children died in the camp, a million of them Jews. Huge numbers died in the gas chambers – the four large chambers were able to put to death about two thousand people at a time – while many others starved to death or were tortured in experiments.

When we look at numbers this vast and horrifying, we can forget that each of the dead was a unique human being with their own unique way of living, their own unique dreams and ambitions, successes and failures. They were all sons and daughters, mothers and fathers, brothers and sisters. Friends and lovers. One of the crimes of Auschwitz was to dehumanize the human.

INTRODUCTION

And in this dehumanizing, we can also forget another human quality which resists every horror and which has always been the greatest weapon against those who live by cruelty and hate. That quality is hope.

We also know now – as Levi could not have, as he and his fellow inmates shared tiny morsels of stale and rancid bread that kept them barely alive – that the Nazis and the Fascists were at this point heading towards defeat, and that their leaders and accomplices were already on their way to justice.

The prisoners were calling on the power of hope. In this book you will read tales of extraordinary bravery and courage, of optimism and endurance, in a place where a small morsel of hope was as vital as those small morsels of bread. You will see men, women and children decide that life is supposed to triumph over death, safe in the knowledge that humans are worth more than what their captors could know, and that every small triumph against despair was another little pebble that would eventually build a wall of resistance far bigger than the barbed wire that surrounded them.

You will also see the ways in which one person's courage can inspire other acts of courage, and that for many who were on the verge of admitting defeat, a simple smile, a helping hand or a shared piece of food gave the strength to carry on. Small gestures of kindness in all of life are golden, but in Auschwitz they were the most valuable commodity of all.

Primo Levi always saw himself as one of the lucky ones – had he been captured earlier, when the camp was at its most ruthless, he would have gone to the chamber. Had he been older or younger, he would have gone too. And there was also, as Levi admitted, an element of luck. He would spend the rest of his life suffering from survivor's guilt.

But he would also spend the rest of his life bearing witness. His books about Auschwitz – *If This Is a Man*, *The Truce*, *The Periodic Table* and *The Drowned and the Saved* – are themselves testaments of hope. By telling the stories of those who died and those who lived – the drowned and the saved – Levi told the story of unquenchable humanity, of triumph in the face of adversity, of hope against despair.

And these are stories we must continue to tell, to remind ourselves not only of the evil in humans, but of the good, and to remind ourselves that good can triumph, but only if it is treasured, nurtured and made real. Hope is the engine of this. As Levi wrote in *If This Is A Man*, we all "possess one power, and we must defend it with all our strength for it is the last – the power to refuse our consent." This is the duty of all of us. He also warned of the human tendency to forget even events as horrifying as the death camps and cautioned those who are quick to neglect the past: "Those who deny Auschwitz would be ready to remake it."

THE HOPE OF HOLDING HER CHILD

Fanny Aizenberg was working when the war came. She was part of a team of designers creating clothes for the Belgian royal family. Born in 1916 in Łódź, in what is now Poland, she emigrated with her family to Belgium when she was ten. One of three children in an Orthodox family, she had earned a degree in art and design before World War Two.

Her husband, a fellow Polish émigré, Jacques "Jack" Aizenberg, was a violinist for silent films and a tailor. The couple had a daughter, Josiane, who was born in 1939. Life seemed good for the Aizenbergs.

Then, in 1940, Nazi Germany invaded Belgium. Jack and his brother fled to England – this was seen as the sensible thing to do, as it was feared that the Nazis would arrest all young men. Jack would join the Polish contingent of the British Army and work in a factory making uniforms in London.

This left the women and children to fend for themselves – and what Fanny and Josiane would face was worse than anything they could have imagined. The Nazis immediately instituted anti-Semitic laws. Jews like Fanny were forbidden to work. Children were thrown out of school. The medical centre where Fanny took Josiane was declared off-limits to anyone of a Jewish background. And all Jews in occupied Belgium had to purchase and wear a yellow star with the letter J on it, identifying them as Jews.

Then, in August 1942, the Nazis began arresting Jews and transporting them to Auschwitz.

Among those taken in the first wave of arrests was Fanny's father, Benjamin Orenbuch, who was employed by the Orthodox community of Brussels that coordinated Jewish activities, such as services and burials. At the time, the world had no idea what was happening at Auschwitz – it may have been a simple internment camp. It was not until after the war that the family heard that Benjamin was dead.

Fanny and her mother, Rivka, spent the next year and a half hiding – Fanny had made the heart-breaking decision to send tiny Josiane away for her safety to a convent in Bruges. She had now lost her father, husband and her daughter. She did what she could to help the Belgian resistance. But in early 1944, Fanny and Rivka were arrested and taken to a Belgian transit camp, where they were both beaten by the Gestapo. And in May 1944, they too were taken to Auschwitz.

Fanny would later describe her first moments there – arriving in the filth and deprivation of a hell on earth. She and Rivka underwent "selection" – the process of deciding who was fit enough to work and who wasn't. Fanny passed and was selected for forced labour in a grenade factory. Rivka failed and was sent to the gas chamber. Fanny saw her mother being dragged away.

THE HOPE OF HOLDING HER CHILD

Where can one find hope in such a situation? For Fanny, it was in friendship. She had five friends in the camp who were in the same situation – they had seen their families destroyed for the "crime" of being Jewish. They had lost children, they had lost parents. They had also all suffered one of the greatest horrors of Auschwitz – invasive medical experiments, on top of the regular beatings.

For Fanny, sharing these horrors with the other women helped her to endure them. As did the hope of seeing her daughter again. Day after day she and the other women would work until they dropped – literally – but when they could, they spoke of times after the camp, when they would live again.

Then, in January 1945, the SS (Schutzstaffel) evacuated the Jews from Auschwitz. But this did not mark the end of the misery. As the Nazi armies crumbled, survivors still in the camps, including Fanny, were forced to march long distances into Germany. The Nazis didn't want them telling of the horrors of the camps when the Allied forces arrived, and they still needed labour for their armaments factories. The SS guards had strict orders to kill those on the "death march" who could no longer walk or travel.

Fanny walked for four months. But in April 1945, as they approached the heart of the Reich, the march was captured by the Soviet army and everyone was held prisoner. The Soviets sorted out the camp survivors from the SS men, and took the prisoners to a makeshift hospital where they were fed and cared for. Soon after, the Red Cross repatriated Fanny to Belgium.

And there she was to have the moment that she had dreamed about, and which had driven her hope – she was reunited with her daughter, Josiane, who had survived in hiding. Her husband, Jack, returned a year later in 1946. He had been badly injured when a bomb had hit his London home.

In 1949, Fanny, Jack and Josiane moved to the United States, and lived in New Jersey. Josiane married Freddie Traum, who had been evacuated from Austria as a nine-year-old. His entire family had been murdered by the Nazis. The couple had three children.

And Fanny? Despite the best efforts of the Nazis, she lived to 102, spending the last years of her life surrounded by grandchildren and great-grandchildren. When she died in 2018, she had lived another 73 years after leaving Auschwitz – and she and her beloved Josiane had seen the Nazi oppressors defeated and those who tried to destroy them consigned to the trash can of history.

ONE THOUSAND DEGREES CELSIUS

He was only 17, but he told them he was 20 so that they would select him for forced labour – rather than risk being sent to his death for being younger and slighter. When John Chillag arrived at Auschwitz in June 1944, he, his father and his uncle were, like all new arrivals, subjected to the selection process. His father and uncle were bound to be judged useful to the Nazis, but the gangly 17-year-old was unsure. He passed, however, and was set to work. The three men were shaved and given prisoner uniforms.

Each of them was also assigned a number which was to replace their name – and was tattooed on their wrist. This chilling example of the Nazi dehumanization of the camp prisoners was unique to Auschwitz – a permanent reminder for those who survived that they had once been regarded as less than animals.

According to the Nazis, John was no longer John. He was 84007.

John, his father and uncle were assigned to work in the camp armaments factory, a form of slave labour during which the workers were mistreated in ways that are barely describable. Denied food and water, and forced to work for hour after hour until they were physically unable to continue, many of them simply wasted away, replaced by other prisoners from a seemingly unlimited supply.

All the time they had no idea what had become of the rest of their family. It was not until after the war that John was to discover that 58 members of his family had been gassed on arrival at Auschwitz. Included in this number was his mother.

For John, the only hope was to work with his body, and escape through daydreams in his mind. No matter how much he lost physically, he could always gain mentally. He could not have dreamed it then, but he would eventually go on to work on intellectual disability issues and teach languages at Leeds Metropolitan University in the UK. The young man literally slaving away at Auschwitz was to keep his mind free well after the Nazis were gone.

After a time at Auschwitz, John and his father were transferred to an armament factory in Bochum in Westphalia to work as forced labourers producing naval cannons. John operated a steel forging press, dealing with metals at 1,000°C (1,832°F). There was no ventilation and no protective clothing. Injury meant death. All the while his mind went back to Auschwitz and the suffering of those still there.

His father died on that factory floor. And the gangly 17-year-old continued to get smaller. As the Nazi regime collapsed, he was taken to another concentration camp, at Buchenwald. On 11 April 1945, John Chillag was one of

ONE THOUSAND DEGREES CELSIUS

21,000 inmates liberated by US forces.

He weighed just 25 kilograms (just under 4 stone). It was not thought he would survive.

But survive he did. And his existence became an act of resistance against what the Nazis had tried to do. He returned to his native Hungary and discovered that his entire family had been killed. When the Soviets took over the country, he left, eventually making his way to Vienna.

There he secured passage to Australia, arriving in 1950. He made a life there, met his wife Audrey and had three children. They emigrated to the UK in 1962, and he found a job as a specialist in German and Italian languages at the British Library in Boston Spa in Yorkshire, before working at Leeds Metropolitan University teaching German and Italian.

The man who had once pretended to be 20 lived to be 81. As well as his work with people with intellectual disabilities, he also spent the last few years of his life speaking to an estimated 20,000 schoolchildren and adult groups throughout the UK and Germany about his Holocaust experiences, and teaching them that no matter what they try to do to your body, hope will always keep your mind free.

THE STRONGER ONES

He had always wanted to be an actor. Born in Vienna in 1912, Hermann Langbein initially chose a life on the stage, but this was cut short by another calling. Always sensitive to injustice, at the age of 21 he joined the Communist Party of Austria, which was banned a year later, leaving him a fugitive. And when Hitler took over Austria in 1938, he fled the country – but not for a life of peace.

Driven by his devotion to fighting fascism in all its forms, Langbein joined the International Brigade in the Spanish Civil War. The war, an intense battle between the left-wing Republicans and the right-wing Nationalists led by General Francisco Franco, was a bloody precursor to the World War that would break out in 1939.

Langbein found himself on the losing side and fled to France, but was captured. Interred in a French prison he seemed destined for a long stay. And then, in 1940, Germany invaded and defeated France. Hermann Langbein was sent to a concentration camp – Dachau.

Originally built for Hitler's political opponents, rather than for Jews, the camp had been in operation since 1933, when Hitler had come to power. It had a reputation for treating prisoners with particular brutality – as active opponents of the Nazis, prisoners in Dachau were routinely tortured as part of their interrogation, and their "re-education". The ancient form of torture known as *strappado*, in which a prisoner has their hands tied behind their back and is suspended by a rope above their heads, dislocating their shoulders, was reintroduced, as were floggings and "standing cells".

Langbein suffered all of this. But, as we shall see, the re-education didn't take.

In 1942, he was transferred to Auschwitz. As a non-Jewish prisoner, he found himself working as a clerk for the garrison physician Dr Eduard Wirths. Wirths was a dedicated anti-Semite, known for carrying out experiments on Jewish prisoners, and was particularly interested in finding ways to sterilize women.

For all that, Langbein would later describe Wirths as an "*anständiger* Nazi" – a decent Nazi – in comparison with other doctors in the camps. It was this decency that Langbein started to work on, gradually convincing Wirths to make conditions better for medical patients and to immunize inmates against typhus.

Langbein would eventually credit Wirths with saving around 93,000 prisoners – a figure calculated from the difference in death rates for the period before and after immunization began. Langbein was assisted by the Austrian nurse Maria Stromberger, who we will encounter later.

Langbein's position also meant that he had access to a great deal of paperwork, detailing the crimes of the Auschwitz medical team, which he managed to copy or steal. He also saw first-hand some of the most gruesome procedures. As a

THE STRONGER ONES

witness, and in providing documentation, Langbein would be key to many of the convictions of those who carried out their deadly work at Auschwitz. Wirths was not included – he had committed suicide on 20 September 1945.

In addition, Langbein and a number of other prisoners formed the Kampfgruppe Auschwitz, a resistance organization with members of various nationalities, which worked to plan escapes, attack guards when possible, and to get information from the camps out to other resistance organizations and then to the wider world.

In 1944 Langbein was again transferred, this time to Neuengamme. He later escaped from an evacuation transport in April 1945. Commandeering a bicycle, he rode back to Vienna, arriving on 5 May, three days before VE Day.

His work to expose the camps had only just begun. First he wrote a book, *Die Stärkeren: Ein Bericht aus Auschwitz und anderen Konzentrationslagern* (*The Stronger Ones: A Report from Auschwitz and Other Concentration Camps*), one of the earliest first-hand accounts exposing many of the true horrors of Auschwitz.

After his return to Vienna, in 1954 he joined other former prisoners in founding the International Auschwitz Committee (IAC). Its task – which it still carries out today – is to support survivors and to fight racism and anti-Semitism.

Throughout his life he continued to campaign for those who had survived the camps, and to seek compensation for the victims of Auschwitz and the families of those who had been killed. He was crucial in helping set up the Frankfurt Auschwitz trials in 1963–68, which led to the convictions of 750 middle ranking SS personnel who had served at Auschwitz.

He was awarded the title Righteous Among the Nations – a title conferred by Yad Vashem, the memorial institution for victims of the Holocaust – for his work. He would outlive Hitler by 50 years, and spent many of those years teaching children and adults about the true horror of Auschwitz.

HE WHO SAVES ONE LIFE

The story of Auschwitz is the story of many tragedies – lives broken and ended by one of the most horrifying events in human history. As we have seen, Auschwitz was also a place where hope refused to die. But the story of Jerzy Bielecki and Cyla Cybulska stands alone. It is a story of tragedy, then love and hope, then tragedy, and then hope again. It is the story of two people who against all odds fell in love, who against all odds escaped, and who against all odds found each other again.

Cyla Cybulska was born on 28 December 1920 in Łomża, a city in Poland, northeast of Warsaw. In her late teens, a portion of the city became a Jewish ghetto, into which she was placed along with her father Mordechai, her mother Fela, an older brother Jakub, a younger brother Natan, and a little sister Rebecca, then ten years old.

In 1942 the ghetto was liquidated, and those who survived were sent to an ex-army barracks in Zambrów, where some 13,000–20,000 prisoners were held. The camp was divided into seven blocks, and conditions were horrific – mortality, according to survivors, was around a hundred a day. Some mothers even killed their own children to save them from suffering.

Survivor Icchak Stupnik wrote in his memoirs that there were three main ways in which people died in the camp – the first was starvation, the second was the cold, and the third was by being beaten for the smallest infraction. In the end, conditions there were too foul and too chaotic even for the Nazis. The camp was liquidated, and those who remained were sent to Birkenau.

Cyla remembered the selection process there – her mother and ten-year-old sister were sent straight to the gas chambers. She was spared and assigned number 29558 by a tattoo on her forearm. Her task was to be hard labour – she and her fellow female inmates were often assigned the job of demolishing the homes and farm buildings of Polish families that had either fled or been murdered.

Soon after, she was sent to Auschwitz and had the somewhat good fortune to be regarded as attractive by the guards – she was one of around 50 women who were given separate lodgings from the other women, an administrative building on the outskirts of the camp. They slept in a dry cellar, were allowed to grow their hair longer and received better food. Their job was to mend burlap sacks for flour at one of the grain warehouses.

Their accommodation also suffered less surveillance than the other parts of the camp – which is what allowed Cyla to meet, and fall in love with, a man named Jerzy Bielecki.

Jerzy Bielecki was a Polish Catholic, born in 1921 in Słaboszów. At the start of the war he joined the Polish army and was captured on 7 May 1940 by the Gestapo. A month later, on 14 June 1940, he was sent to the newly created Auschwitz concentration camp with the first transport of 728 Polish political prisoners – the low number tattooed on his forearm, 243, reflects how early he arrived there. It is possible that he was the prisoner with the lowest number to survive Auschwitz.

He was assigned work in the same grain warehouse where Cyla was mending sacks. Despite the fact that men and women were not allowed to talk to each other, the two managed to exchange a few words every day through a hole in the wall between her work area and his. They also exchanged letters – secret notes known in the camp as "gyps". This was a clandestine activity in Auschwitz, and the penalty for being caught was death. But the two lovers carried on passing their notes, and on more than one occasion were able to kiss each other through the hole in the wall. Jerzy would later say that they were like teenagers stealing kisses as death rumbled all around them.

Sometimes death was closer than was bearable. Cyla would recall that one of her best friends was standing beside her when a Nazi approached, put a revolver to her neck and shot her dead – for no reason at all. It could have been Cyla. When she told Jerzy this, he made a momentous decision – one which many of the inmates of Auschwitz had no doubt made, but almost none had managed to carry out. He was going to escape. He said to Cyla that he would save her from the hellhole of the camp. "For Cyla and our love I was prepared to do anything," he later said.

In this he was assisted by his good friend, Tadeusz Srogi, who somehow managed to have himself transferred to a part of the camp where Nazi uniforms were kept. One was stolen for Jerzy and hidden away until the right time.

On 21 July 1944, they decided to make their move. They needed a day pass to get out, and forgers within the camp had made copies of these in the various colours, as a new colour was randomly chosen for each day This day was green. Jerzy ran off to get his pass and put on the uniform. He then went and found Cyla and pretended to be a guard taking her away.

She would later say that as they walked to the gates, her fear was "genuine". Jerzy passed through the various identification checks, even forcing himself to say "*Heil* Hitler" to approaching guards. At the control box his papers were checked and he was waved through with his Jewish prisoner. He expected at every moment to feel a bullet in his back. None came. They had made it.

Cyla was, as far as can be ascertained, the only Jewish woman ever to escape from Auschwitz, and only the sixth Jew to do so. The pair walked for ten days. At one point they passed an SS man who knew both of them but failed to recognize the escapees. Jerzy carried Cyla over rivers, and at night they slept wherever they could hide in an area now fully populated by Nazis. Finally they arrived at their destination, the house of Jerzy's uncle in Przemęczany in southern Poland, where his mother was also living.

By this point Cyla was totally exhausted, and when Jerzy decided to go on to Kraków to find a way forward for them both, he left her behind in the care of his family. Both would later recall that night, kissing goodbye under a pear tree.

HE WHO SAVES ONE LIFE

After the Soviet army rolled through Kraków in January 1945, Jerzy left the city, where he had been hiding from the Nazis, and walked 40 kilometres (25 miles) along snow-covered roads to return to Cyla at the farmhouse. But he arrived four days too late. Cyla had received news that he had been killed and had left for Warsaw, eventually finding safety in Sweden. On the train, she met a Jewish man, David Zacharowitz, and the two began a relationship. They eventually married and started a jewellery business. Zacharowitz died in 1975.

Jerzy meanwhile tried to find his love, but in the chaos of the aftermath of the war, where people were crossing countries and changing names (as were the countries), he was unsuccessful. He became a motor mechanic and also married.

After the night under the pear tree, they were not to see each other for 40 years.

It was in May 1983, in New York, that Cyla learned that Jerzy was alive and well, when a Polish woman cleaning her family's apartment mentioned a documentary in which she had seen his story. Cyla called him. "It's me, your little Cyla," she said. They exchanged letters, and on 8 June 1983 they met each other in Poland.

According to Jerzy they fell back in love, but he would not leave his wife and son. Some have said she cut off relations with him at that point, but according to family friends they met up at least a dozen more times and remained friends. Cyla passed away in 2005.

Jerzy co-founded and became the honorary chairman of the Christian Association of Auschwitz Families. He was also inscribed on the list of the Righteous Among the Nations in 1985. His autobiography was called *He Who Saves One Life* after the quote from the Talmud, "He who saves one life saves a whole world." He died in 2011. On his death bed he said of his relationship with Cyla, "It's fate that decided things that way. But if I could do it again I wouldn't change anything."

SMALL ACTS OF KINDNESS

She was only a small teenager, but that didn't matter. When Edith Rubin was sent to Auschwitz she had to do backbreaking work like everyone else.

Edith was born in Hungary, in a village so small that her phone number was "2". Her family were forced to move by growing anti-Semitism. Then, when she was 15, the trains came, and she was taken to Auschwitz, separated from her family and had her head shaved.

Her work was to dig. The inmates often had to walk long distances to where they would spend the day shovelling the hard earth, and there was a very simple rule that each of them knew – if you became too sick or tired to do the work, you were no longer needed. You were sent to the gas chamber.

Edith worked hard, but then one day, she injured her leg. The wound began to fester. She started to limp. As the inmates marched to where they would be digging, she struggled at each and every step. To fall meant death.

It was then that another prisoner stepped in. Edith did not know her name and would never learn it – but that woman carried her shovel for her each day until the wound healed.

"She took from me the shovel, and said, 'I want to do it'… and when I saw this kindness, then I imagined I had some hope," Edith told Boston's WBUR radio in 2020.

This was not the only small act of kindness she recalled – there was one German officer, she said, who every day would surreptitiously place his lunch on the ground and walk away without looking back. It was for the inmates.

That Edith was able to tell her story is a miracle in itself. In early 1945, Denmark managed to negotiate the release of thousands of prisoners from the concentration camps. Edith was one of these. Initially, she returned to Hungary, and later emigrated to the US, where she had two daughters and three grandchildren.

All of them owe their lives to these small acts of kindness.

BREADCRUMBS

"Five hundred and ninety-nine women would line up every day to give me a crumb of their bread." – Fritzie Fritzshall

She was a 13-year-old girl living in her hometown of Klucharky, formerly in Czechoslovakia, when they came for her, her mother and two younger brothers. Her father had moved to Illinois the year before to earn money to send back to the family. The Nazis were thorough – for Fritzie Fritzshall and her family there was no possibility of escaping the cattle car which would take them across Poland to their final destination: Auschwitz.

Fritzie later described her arrival at the camp to the Jewish Women's Archive – the bright light shone into the darkness of the train compartment, the loudspeakers giving orders in a language she didn't understand. One Jewish prisoner whispered to the new arrivals in Yiddish, "Say you are 15… say you are 15." Fifteen was an age at which you could work – under 15 meant the gas chamber.

She was immediately separated from her family, including of course her mother, who was deemed too old to work.

"When I asked several hours later when I would see her," Fritzie recalled, "they pointed to the smoke." She was already dead.

Fritzie had her head shaved, and then began work at a labour camp, making aeroplane parts. She was one of 600 women working there, and she was the youngest. All the other women made a decision that would save her life.

Each of them, every day, gave her a crumb from their small piece of bread – 599 pieces in all. As the youngest, it was thought she was most likely to survive, and this daily offering would help her do that. Only one thing was asked of her in return – that when this hell was over, she would go out into the world and tell their stories. And that they be remembered when challah – the Jewish ceremonial bread – is eaten.

Fritzie Fritzshall did survive. In 1945, she was liberated by the Soviet Army after escaping into a nearby forest during a death march. These death marches were as grotesque as the camps themselves, as she later described. The Germans, losing the war, had no idea what to do with their prisoners, so they marched them from place to place, without food or water. As they passed through villages, sometimes a window would open and a loaf of bread or a potato would be thrown to the starving inmates.

After the war, Fritzie had stories to tell.

A passionate advocate of Holocaust testimony, she spent her life dedicated to reminding the world of the horrors that she, and so many other women, men and children, suffered at the hands of the Nazis. She eventually became president of the Illinois Holocaust Museum and Education Center in

BREADCRUMBS

Skokie, having emigrated to the US to find her father.

She knew how easy it is for normal people to engage in evil, and during the 1970s organized a rally against neo-Nazis in Illinois. What's more, she persuaded the governor, James Thompson, to sign the first Holocaust Education Mandate into law, making Illinois the first state in the country to require the teaching of the Holocaust in all schools.

Fritzie also knew, from those women who gave up their bread, how easy it is for people to be drawn to good – but that vigilance is essential. As she put it in a 2019 interview, "'Never again' must be 'never again'. It must stop."

THE ELEVENTH COMMANDMENT

They are some of the most famous marches in history against racial segregation: Martin Luther King Jr's marches from Selma to Montgomery, US in 1965. Thousands of people of all races, colours and creeds marched for equality and shared King's dream of their children not being judged "by the colour of their skin but by the content of their character".

Among the marchers was a man who had seen first-hand the horrors of discrimination based on race – Auschwitz survivor Marian Turski.

Turski was born Moshe Turbowicz in Druskininkai, in what was then Poland but is now part of Lithuania. After the Nazis conquered Poland in 1940, he and his family were moved to the Jewish ghetto established in Łódź, which was plagued by disease, starvation and forced labour. He was one of a peak population of 163,777 "residents", which gradually and then rapidly depleted as they were sent to the death camps.

Turski, his father and brother were deported to Auschwitz in August 1944 – as with so many others, they were crowded together in a cattle truck, barely able to move, without any food and water for the 270-kilometre (168-mile) journey.

Turski's father was already ageing before they left, while his brother became sick on the way to the camp. When they disembarked, Turski was sent to the line for those who could work – he was now prisoner B-940. His father and brother were sent to the line for the gas chambers. He would never see them again – they were killed within hours of reaching the camp.

Turski would spend the next five months carrying out hard labour, in the certain knowledge that his father and brother were dead. It was one of the most harrowing aspects of the Nazis' cruelty that those who were not chosen for execution spent their days in the shadow of the crematoria chimneys – a constant reminder of those they had lost, and a looming threat of what their own fate might be.

In January 1945, Turski was sent on the death march and then by freight train to Buchenwald. Some 60,000 men were on the march, and some 15,000 of them died. When Turski was finally liberated, he was afflicted by malnutrition and typhus. He would later say that he experienced amnesia for 20 years – certain episodes at Auschwitz remained with him, while the rest had been blocked out, only slowly returning over time. He was not sure what was worse – the forgetting or the remembering.

He would later, in a speech to the United Nations (UN) in 2019, consider the question he was asked the most about Auschwitz – what was the worst thing about it?

Was it, he said, the hunger? Turski recounted that all day, every day he was haunted by the spectre of a potato, a spoonful of soup, a bite of bread. If you have not suffered that sort of hunger – he compared it to what people were suffering at the time in the Sudan and Yemen – you cannot know what it is like. But the worst thing wasn't the hunger.

Was it the cold? The winter of 1944 was especially frigid, often getting down to −20°C (−4°F), and the prison uniforms they wore were not only thin but also full of holes – they were virtually rags. He told the story of being accused by the Nazi guards of stealing German property when the underclothes he had made out of cement bags showed through his uniform. The underwear was torn from him and he was given a savage beating, and sent back to work. But the worst thing wasn't the cold.

Was it, as he put it with irony, the "living conditions"? Turski described what it was like to live in barracks that housed up to 1,200 people. The prisoners were made to sleep in bunks of five, six or even seven people to a bed. They had to fight for their choice of top or bottom bunk. The advantage of the top bunk was that you avoided being under the leaking bladder of another man – there were no easily accessed toilet facilities in the night – and waking up soaked in urine. But if there was a roll call, which happened randomly but frequently, it was much harder to get from the bed to where the numbers were being counted off. Such was the exhaustion of the inmates, that getting in and out of bed could prove fatal. So to choose either the top or bottom bunk was to face a night of horror. But, said Turski, the worst thing wasn't the "living conditions".

Was it the lice? He didn't remember lice at Auschwitz, but he did remember them being everywhere else, including in a factory that had been destroyed that the inmates were sent to clean up. They were everywhere, and the men had no facilities for washing them off. And then later, during the death march from Auschwitz, there were millions of them. They were more than just an irritant – they were unbearable. The deaths of some among the quarter of the marchers who perished could be attributed to the constant presence of lice, spreading not only typhus but a sense of helplessness and depression, such that some of the marchers could not go on. But still, they were not the worst thing.

So, what was the worst thing? The worst thing, Marian Turski told the UN, was the humiliation. For being Jewish, and only for being Jewish, the Nazi regime and the guards treated the inmates, in Turski's words, like lice, like bed bugs, like cockroaches. And what do people do to lice, bed bugs and cockroaches? They crush them and kill them.

So, for all the physical hardship, it was this mental hardship that Turski, like so many others, felt most acutely and was the worst thing about Auschwitz. That was why Turski delivered a simple message to the UN about how to ensure it never happened again: the antidote to humiliation is empathy and compassion.

It was not just when talking to the UN that Turski would promote these values. The whole of his life after Auschwitz was spent advocating for ways to prevent what the Nazis did ever happening again. He studied history at the University of Wrocław, in Poland, during which time he took up journalism and worked in political communications. He then worked for political parties that attempted to stop Stalin from taking control of Poland. In 1958, he became editor of the magazine *Polityka*'s history section. He went on to become an influential journalist and historian, and as we have seen, in 1965 attended the freedom marches of Martin Luther King while on a government scholarship to the US.

He also became vice-president of the Jewish Historical Institute in Poland, and a member of the governing board of the Association of Jewish Combatants and Victims of World War Two. Both organizations fought against the forces that had shaped National Socialism by providing testimony about the Holocaust and bearing witness to its horrors. He received letters of congratulation from Chancellor Angela Merkel of Germany and US president Barack Obama in 2016, on his ninetieth birthday.

Age had not wearied Turski – after the UN speech, he spoke at the 75th anniversary of the Liberation of Auschwitz, aged 93. He reiterated his message of empathy and compassion, introducing what he called the Eleventh Commandment – do not be indifferent. Auschwitz, he said, did not fall from the sky, and if it could happen there at that time, it could happen anywhere at any time.

Marian dedicated his life to conserving the history of Poland's Jews, converting his traumatic past into action to provide a small measure of justice to the victims of the Holocaust. When he died at the age of 98 in early 2025, tributes poured in from around the world. Poland's chief rabbi, Michael Schudrich, said the Jewish community would miss Mr Turski greatly. "Marian was our teacher, he was our moral voice and mentor," he said. And a beacon of hope, now and forever.

ONE SUNDAY AFTERNOON IN AUSCHWITZ

They were sisters, born 14 months apart. Agnes Laszlo was born on 2 June 1930, and her sister Zsuzsanna in September 1931, in Miskolc, Hungary. It was not until 19 March 1944, nearly five years into the war, that the Germans finally occupied Hungary, but the result was immediately the same – Jews like Agi and Zsuzsanna, their father, Zoltan and mother Rosza were rounded up.

The shock was too much for Zoltan – already suffering from an illness, he died that very day. The two girls and their mother were transported to Auschwitz, and to the unbelievable horrors of human depravity. That they managed to stick together was a miracle in itself.

By this point Germany was increasingly in chaos, and the three were moved to Płaszów concentration camp in Kraków, and then when that shut down, returned to Auschwitz – almost certainly to die. How could they continue to hope?

It was on a Sunday afternoon, Agi remembered, that they heard a remarkable sound. It was, she said, a particularly dismal day when she was starving and weak from exhaustion.

Then one of the women, from the same small town as the girls, stood up. And began to sing.

Known only as Lili, she sang arias from operas – *La Bohème*, *Tosca*, *Madame Butterfly*. "It was hard to believe," said Agi, "that such a beautiful and powerful voice could emerge from such a tiny, frail young woman."

Everyone was transfixed and many people cried – including the guards. Agi said she was mesmerized by the music, that it replenished her supply of hope – the most precious commodity, she later said, one could have in Auschwitz.

This was the first Sunday on which Lili sang, but not the last. Week after week she would sing for the inmates, but many of the Nazi guards would also come to hear her. For someone like Agi, it was something to look forward to all week – a reason to live.

Music has long been intertwined with the Jewish life, in religious ceremonies, and as part of the secular community. There is also a long tradition of Jewish composers and musicians in the classical realm, including opera. Here was another link to Jewish tradition entering into camp life and ameliorating it.

Soon after, Agi, Zsuzsanna and Rosza were selected to be transferred to a labour camp in Rochlitz, near Leipzig, in Germany, to make aeroplane parts, taking them away from Lili's music. But they could never forget it. The family were then moved to another factory in Calw, near Stuttgart, and when it closed down they were sent on a death march, but they were saved by American troops on 28 April 1945. They stayed in Innsbruck in Austria for eight months, before going back to Hungary, and then in 1949 to Israel. Agi had two children, and Zsuzsanna married a fellow survivor and had three. Their mother, Rosza, remarried and followed them to Israel, passing away at the age of 98.

But the mystery of Lili remained. That was until Agi, having moved to America, decided to use the archives of the Holocaust Memorial Museum to see if she could track Lili down. She did. Lili was still alive. And living just 8 kilometres (5 miles) away from her. They met up soon after and remained friends.

The mystery was solved, and the wonder remained. Agi would say that for the rest of her life, the memory of that voice raised in song would still make her shiver. Truly a story of hope.

PRISONER 107984

"We have been saved, but we are not liberated." – Norbert Wollheim, 26 August 1945

Norbert Wollheim would later say that when the train left Berlin, with him, his sister Ruth, his wife Rosa and their three-year-old son Peter on board, the general feeling was one of relief and expectation. Trains had been departing from Berlin for months, and the waiting for their number to come up had been stressful in itself. But finally, Norbert and his family were going off to meet their fate.

What that fate was they could not be sure – probably a labour camp who knows where, they thought, where they would serve their time before either being released or repatriated. He and his wife noticed the train was heading east and remembered travelling the same route on their honeymoon to Silesia. Rosa wrote a few postcards – they knew that previous passengers had thrown postcards from the windows and they had been picked up and mailed by well-meaning Germans.

One of the older women on the train noted it was a Friday evening, a night of worship for Jews, and had brought candles with her, which she lit, and started saying the prayers. Wollheim said it was a comfort to all of them, and there was mostly a feeling of anticipation. What they did not know as they prayed that evening was that 95 per cent of the people on that train would not live to see the next evening. Their destination was Auschwitz.

Norbert Wollheim was a true Berliner. Born on 26 April 1913, he had studied jurisprudence and political economy at university, but he had to end his studies when Hitler came to power in 1933. For the next six years he worked as a welder for a metal export firm.

But he was also fully engaged in Judaism and politics, and the point where they met. Deeply influenced by the Jewish youth movement of the 1920s and 1930s, he was active in community work, which in 1938–39 would come to include helping to organize the Kindertransport which sent Jewish German children to safety in Britain. In 1939, he also personally accompanied Kindertransports to Sweden, but he immediately returned to Berlin after leaving the children in safety. His own son Peter was born that year.

He spent much of the next three years living on his wits. In a Berlin draped in Nazi swastikas and where Jewish businesses were being burned to the ground, this was not easy. On 8 March the four members of the Wollheim family were arrested and taken to the train station.

Of the 95 per cent who didn't see the next evening, three were Wollheim's sister, wife and son. While he was being assessed for physical labour, they were being taken to the gas chamber and murdered.

PRISONER 107984

Wollheim passed his physical and was sent to the Buna/Monowitz concentration camp to perform forced labour for IG Farben at the construction site in Auschwitz.

Founded in 1925, IG Farbenindustrie AG was one of the leading chemical corporations of the interwar period. Under the Nazis, the conglomerate played a major part in the Third Reich's policy of rearmament. In the 1940s the company relied on slave labour from concentration camps, including 30,000 prisoners from Auschwitz, and one of its subsidiaries supplied the poison gas Zyklon B, used in the gas chambers.

And that was not all – they were also heavily involved in human experimentation, deliberately infecting inmates, mostly women, with typhoid, tuberculosis, diphtheria and other diseases, and then testing their drugs on them.

In one awful example, they paid 150 Reichsmarks (RM) per woman for 150 women from Auschwitz – which they had haggled down from 200 RM – in order to test an anaesthetic. The final report said that the 150 women "arrived in good condition". However, they were unable to obtain "conclusive results" because the women "died during the experiments". They "kindly requested" that another group of women be sent, the same number, "at the same price". It is assumed they were sent.

Wollheim worked at IG Farben's factory Buna/Monowitz, constructing the materials for a new rubber-producing factory – but it was never built. On 18 January 1945, Auschwitz was evacuated, and on one of the death marches of camp inmates being evacuated, Wollheim managed to flee.

He returned to Germany, settling in the northern city of Lübeck, then under British occupation. His mission was to help rebuild the Jewish community in West Germany from the ruins that had been left by the Nazis. But he also had another aim, which was to change the law, not only in Germany, and not only in terms of the Holocaust. He wanted IG Farben to be held responsible for their crimes, both legally and financially. He wanted restitution.

After the war, 24 of the directors had been put on trial. Thirteen defendants were found guilty with sentences ranging from 18 months to eight years, but most were released early, and several of them returned to high management positions. And while IG Farben was ordered to be liquidated, it managed to be "in liquidation" for the next 50 years, with all its assets transferred to the smaller companies of which it was composed.

Wollheim's suit was the first test case of a former forced labourer against a company in Germany. Wollheim and his lawyer, Henry Ormond, sought only 10,000 Deutschmarks (DM) (around £4,000) compensation. The case became a sensation – and was quickly regarded by victims of the Holocaust as the first step in true financial acknowledgement of and compensation for their suffering, and by many German companies as a dangerous precedent. Was going about your business in Nazi Germany collaboration in the Holocaust?

IG Farben's defence arguments were several. First, they claimed not to have known that they were employing slave labour. Second, they claimed that by providing the work, they were saving those they "employed" from a worse fate

PRISONER 107984

– the gas chamber, or simply starving in Auschwitz. Third, they said it was only the SS that mistreated the prisoners – no IG Farben employee was directly involved in any of the brutal treatment. And finally, they argued that the economic system was under the Nazi government, who therefore bore full responsibility. IG Farben had merely worked with what there was.

The trial began in November 1951. It is hard to imagine the state of Norbert Wollheim. He may have been fighting for financial restitution, but thoughts of his dead sister, wife and son cannot have been far from his mind. The urge to scream at the defence witnesses must have been overwhelming. This was no doubt made all the worse by the way the defence witnesses acted – the judges noted the "appalling indifference of the accused" in their final judgement.

These witnesses made the factory sound like a holiday resort, but first-hand accounts of the forced labour told a different story – the words "hell on earth" were repeated several times by men whose physical disabilities were still visible.

Wollheim won the case – but IG Farben appealed, only to lose twice more in 1954. By then a number of other survivors had contacted Henry Ormond, and a class action began. Throughout, IG Farben, supported by other businesses, tried to negotiate outside the court, mostly in order to avoid setting a precedent in law that German companies were responsible for what had happened under Nazi Germany.

In February 1957, an agreement out of court was finally reached – IG Farben agreed to pay 30 million DM to the victims. Of this, 3 million was to go to non-Jewish victims.

The other 27 million was then distributed among 5,900 survivors, who received a payment of around 5,000 DM apiece.

Was this fair compensation for all that suffering, and for the loss of so many family members? Obviously not. But it did set a precedent for businesses to have to act ethically whatever the political situation, and it opened a way for other German businesses that had exploited the Holocaust, and profited from it, to pay – financially at least.

Wollheim emigrated to the US in September 1951 and settled in New York City, where he studied to become an accountant, mostly working pro bono for organizations like the US Holocaust Memorial Council and the World Federation of Bergen-Belsen Survivors.

In 2008, ten years after his death, the Norbert Wollheim Memorial was opened in Frankfurt am Main. A pavilion shows portraits of former prisoners in Buna/Monowitz. Above the entrance is Wollheim's prisoner number, 107984, and inside is his famous quote from the trial, *"Wir sind gerettet, aber wir sind nicht befreit"* – "We are saved but not liberated".

Hope may have come too late for those who perished in Auschwitz, but Norbert Wollheim had given hope to all those in the future – some liberation can come.

THE COOKBOOK

It is so thin and fragile that one can barely touch it. And yet it is as heavy with meaning as any book can possibly be.

When Steven Fenves and his family were being led away in May 1944 from their home in Subotica in what was then Yugoslavia, the 13-year-old boy was shocked to be surrounded by neighbours and other townspeople, who were waiting for them to leave in order to loot their home. The Fenves family were wealthy, and the people in the neighbourhood were only too glad to take away their things.

What Steven and his family didn't notice in the rush of people, was someone known to them – their former cook Maris, who had worked for them until 1941, when new laws made it illegal for Jews to employ non-Jews. As valuables were pulled off shelves and furniture wheeled out, there was only one thing Maris wanted to get hold of. She was not there to loot the property, she was there to save something priceless – the Fenves family cookbook.

This had been put together over many years by Steven's mother, an aunt, a sister and various cousins. Handwritten, changed and adjusted over the years, it had been the mother lode of recipes which Maris drew on to feed the Fenves family.

While she was recovering the book, Steven Fenves had begun his journey to Auschwitz. The trip took five days, crammed into a cattle truck without food or water. As soon as they arrived, his grandmother was taken to the gas chamber, and his mother was killed soon after. Despite his youth, Steven started working with the resistance, helping to organize the black market, trading in gold watches which had been recovered from the dead. As he told the *Washington Post* in 2022, his greatest triumph was to trade for a stick of margarine which he gave to his sister – only to find out later she had eaten it in one sitting and become violently ill.

In April 1945, Steven was sent on a death march. For 11 days, he and fellow inmates marched without being given any food and water, and many of them died. He made the mistake of talking back to a German soldier and had his arm broken. But he survived.

When he and his sister returned to Subotica, all of their treasured possessions were gone – except one. The cookbook. Maris handed it back to them. But Yugoslavia under the Soviets made their life unsafe again, and so they fled for America, leaving the book again in Maris's safekeeping. In 1960 she sent it to them, and it was donated to the Holocaust Memorial Museum.

The book was unique to Steven – but similar books were treasured by many of the families who went through Auschwitz. Cookbooks were a way of archiving their lives, and while the Fenves cookbook predated the camps, many were created on scraps of paper within the camps

THE COOKBOOK

themselves. The Holocaust Memorial Museum has archived at least 30 such books.

It may seem paradoxical that people who were starving should spend their time thinking about food and writing down their family recipes. But, for many, this was exactly what hope was – keeping the thread alive of what came before Auschwitz, with the longing that what would come after would remain part of the tradition. As Kyra Schuster, art and artefacts curator at the Holocaust Memorial Museum put it, "But it was something that kind of kept them grounded, kept their humanity."

Since the book was returned, Steven Fenves has had the opportunity to taste some of the recipes from his childhood – a reminder of a world that may well have been lost, but can now be passed down through the centuries. A thin book, heavy with meaning.

THE SPY

To the guards and commanders at Auschwitz-Birkenau, he was Tomasz Serafiński, prisoner number 4859, as would be tattooed on his wrist. He had arrived in September 1940 and was considered to be just another young male Jew to be used in forced labour until he died or was exterminated.

But Tomasz Serafiński was not Tomasz Serafiński, nor was he Jewish. His real name was Cavalry Captain Witold Pilecki, he was a member of the Polish resistance movement and he was in Auschwitz because he had volunteered to go there – knowing that the price he might have to pay was death.

Born in 1901, and descended from nobility, Pilecki had fought in the Polish–Soviet War of 1919–1920, defending his homeland against the newly installed Communist government of Russia. After the war he inherited the family estates, married and had two children. While rising up the armed forces he indulged his passion for poetry and painting, and he started a horseman training programme. He was becoming part of the leisured class.

And then the war came.

Mobilized at the age of 38, Pilecki found himself on the front line, fighting the German invasion. The battle lasted less than a month, before Germany completely overran Poland. Ordered with the rest of the army to escape via Romania, Pilecki and a few fellow soldiers decided instead to go underground, forming the first Polish resistance organization, Tajna Armia Polska – the Secret Polish Army.

Even at this early stage, rumours had begun to circulate about what was going on in Auschwitz. Pilecki volunteered to try and infiltrate by what seemed to be the only possible method: being arrested. This he did, using the identity papers of an army commander named Tomasz Serafiński, whom he believed to be dead.

It is not clear how much Pilecki knew about what went on in Auschwitz – perhaps no one could truly imagine Auschwitz in a time before Auschwitz – but it was still an act of unbelievable courage. We can only imagine his feeling as the train drew into the camp. If he thought this was going to be a normal prisoner-of-war camp, he would have quickly realized it was something far different.

He immediately began setting up what would be known as the Związek Organizacji Wojskowej (ZOW) – the Military Organization Union – made up of inmates in cells of five people, spread across the camp. The ZOW's activities included distributing contraband food and clothing, providing news from outside to those inside, and news from those inside to those outside, and raising morale.

But it was also a paramilitary organization – members were trained in combat, ready to be activated if the right moment arose, and learned how to drive trains in preparation for a

THE SPY

mass escape, should one be organized. Intelligence networks were also set up to share information.

Pilecki's reports were some of the first to emerge from Auschwitz. In his dispatches to the Home Army – the main resistance movement in Poland – he told of the unbelievable horror of the treatment of prisoners, including the lack of food, the use of torture and, for the first time, the existence of the gas chambers.

Somehow, he and his fellow ZOW members were even able to build a radio transmitter within the camp – it took seven months to build, using parts smuggled in from outside, or made in secret in the various workshops. Pilecki was finally able to broadcast directly to the various resistance organizations inside Poland and further afield. Pilecki believed that the camp could be overrun, and he pleaded – in vain – for troops and ammunition.

As the activities of the ZOW became bolder, the suspicions of the guards grew, and in March and April 1943 many of its members were killed. Pilecki decided to escape, in the hope of rousing the Home Army to take action.

Somehow, on the night of 26–27 April 1943, Pilecki and two fellow resistance fighters managed to get away, overpowering a guard and fleeing with a number of incriminating documents about the activities in the camp. Despite being shot at a number of times and being wounded at least once by bullets, he made it to the town of Bochnia, which had seen its large Jewish population murdered, and which was now a place where secret resistance organizations gathered.

In a remarkable coincidence, Pilecki made contact with the man who ran the resistance movement there and who guided him to a safe house – Commander Tomasz Serafiński, the very man whose identity he had stolen.

Pilecki's pleas to the Home Army – and to the Soviet Red Army which had found itself near Auschwitz – to liberate the camp fell on deaf ears. Both armies felt that any attack would fail, and also that even a successful attack would end up a failure, as they had no capacity for housing or feeding the survivors, let alone getting them out of German-occupied Poland.

For Pilecki, that was the end of his battle over Auschwitz, but not his work for the resistance. As well as continuing to fight, including being part of the Warsaw Uprising in 1944 that attempted without success to throw the Nazis out of Poland, he was known to contribute large sums of money to Jewish resistance groups.

In the end, it was not the Nazis who killed Pilecki – it was the Soviets who had once been his allies in the battle against Hitler. After the war, he was no happier that Poland was under Soviet control than he had been that it was under the National Socialists. He continued his resistance activities, but he was arrested on 8 May 1947 – the second anniversary of VE Day – tortured (he gave away no names) and sentenced to death. A number of Auschwitz survivors, including the Polish prime minister Józef Cyrankiewicz, pleaded for clemency. They were ignored. On 25 May 1947, Pilecki was shot in the back of the head, and buried in an unmarked grave.

Since the fall of the Soviet Union in 1989, Pilecki's bravery has been celebrated. As Poland's chief rabbi put it in 2012,

THE SPY

"When God created the human being, God had in mind that we should all be like Captain Witold Pilecki."

THE CELLIST OF AUSCHWITZ: PART ONE

Music has always been an integral part of the Jewish experience, be it the religious music that is sung at services and ceremonies, or forms such as klezmer, the Ashkenazi tradition with its ritual melodies and taste for improvisation.

In Western classical music, the Jewish tradition has been particularly strong, from Felix Mendelssohn and Gustav Mahler, through to composers such as Philip Glass and Steve Reich. Reich himself has written music memorializing the Holocaust, such as *Different Trains*, which compares his own childhood train journeys in the United States with those that the Jews of Europe were suffering at the same time.

But it is perhaps as performers of classical music that the Jewish tradition is strongest, particularly in string instruments.

The names are numerous. Yehudi Menuhin, Itzhak Perlman, Isidore Cohen, Jascha Heifetz and Isaac Stern are among the greatest names ever to play violin. While Mischa Maisky, Gregor Piatigorsky, Emanuel Feuermann and János Starker are among the greatest performers to ever pick up the cello – perhaps to perform *Kol Nidrei*, the famous cello concerto written by Max Bruch, which uses the melody of the Kol Nidre declaration, sung by the cantor at the start of the Yom Kippur service of atonement.

To that list can be added the name of Anita Lasker-Wallfisch, generally regarded as one of the greatest cellists of all time. Her career would be remarkable enough in isolation, but one fact about Lasker-Wallfisch makes it even more astonishing – she is a survivor of Auschwitz.

She was born Anita Lasker in 1925 in what was then known as Breslau, a German city which is now Wrocław in southwest Poland. Her father was a lawyer, her mother a violinist, and her uncle a chess master, and she had two sisters, Marianne and Renate. Her father had fought for Germany in World War One and received an Iron Cross for bravery. This would later make the family believe that they would be safe when the Nazis came to power. They soon learned that no one Jewish was safe.

Their life was, she would later say, one of culture, where classics were read every Saturday afternoon and there was "a great deal of chamber music" played. In addition, on Sundays the family only spoke French.

But already, while Anita was at school, anti-Semitism was growing. As she relates, "I was about to wipe the blackboard and one of the children said, 'Don't give the Jew the sponge.'" She was also spat at in the street.

In addition, Anita was unable to learn cello, as there were no Jewish cello teachers left in Breslau – they had all been taken – and no non-Jewish teacher would risk teaching a Jew. She was briefly able to go to Berlin to study, but as

THE CELLIST OF AUSCHWITZ: PART ONE

persecution of Jews increased in the capital – synagogues being burned down, lynchings happening in broad daylight – she was forced to return home and, with her remaining family, attempt to get out of Germany.

In 1939, as war began, Anita's older sister was saved by being sent to England as part of the Kindertransport. The rest of the family suffered the persecution that Jews in Nazi Germany were forced to endure; gradually the net was tightening. In 1942, Anita's parents were taken away – she, then 16, and Renate volunteered to go with them, but their father would not let them. The girls never saw their parents again, but later research showed they had been killed after being forced to dig their own graves.

Soon after, the girls' aunt, uncle and grandmother were also taken, never to be heard of again. At the time, the sisters were working in a paper factory, and did what they could to produce forged papers for French prisoners of war to help them escape. They also made papers for themselves. But the German secret police – the Gestapo – was tracking their activities, and Anita was arrested as she tried to flee and charged with forgery. As she later noted, being arrested for a crime spared her the concentration camp for a year – she was held in a normal prison.

It also meant that when she did arrive at Auschwitz, she was not sent for selection like other Jews – as a convicted criminal she was immediately sent to work, as was Renate. They had also been spared the horrors of cattle trains – they had arrived on separate prison trains. But as they watched the smoke rise from the chimneys of the crematoria, there could be little doubt what fate awaited them.

STORIES OF HOPE FROM AUSCHWITZ

In the meantime, there was music – and Anita Lasker became a member of one of the most remarkable groups ever assembled, the Women's Orchestra of Auschwitz, whose story is one of the most extraordinary in all of the history of Auschwitz, as we shall now see.

> See page 69 for part two of Anita's story.

THE WOMEN'S ORCHESTRA OF AUSCHWITZ

The story of the Women's Orchestra of Auschwitz is in many ways the story of Alma Rosé. She was a niece of the famous composer and conductor Gustav Mahler, and her father was the renowned violinist Arnold Rosé, but that did nothing to save Alma from the concentration camp. In 1943, aged 37, she was sent to Auschwitz.

It is possible that when she arrived she shared the experience of another prisoner, 13-year-old Pearl Pufeles, who was astonished that as she disembarked from the train she could hear the sound of classical music, Dvořák and Smetana. Pearl would say after the war that her initial reaction was that Auschwitz couldn't be all that bad if they allowed such music.

The Women's Orchestra of Auschwitz had in fact been started on the orders of the SS, for their own pleasure and as a propaganda tool. Newsreels showing the orchestra playing were broadcast worldwide as a smokescreen for what was really happening in the camp. The woman in charge of the women's camp, Maria Mandl, later executed for her crimes, was tasked with finding players.

Polish music teacher Zofia Czajkowska volunteered to organize and to conduct. Originally, the orchestra only had access to a guitar, a mandolin and percussion instruments, and it was difficult to bring everyone together to rehearse. Sheet music was almost non-existent. But over time, the number of instruments and the repertoire increased. None of the orchestra was allowed relief from their work schedules, so the playing was in addition to these, leading to great exhaustion. But for some, playing gave a feeling of freedom that made up for the extra physical labour.

Much of the music they were forced to play was not joyful – the SS demanded that they play mostly German marching songs, polkas and waltzes. Worse still, they were forced to play at the gate of the women's camp when the work gangs left and returned. They might also play during "selection" for the gas chambers, and as the inmates were being led to their deaths – a grim and sickening reminder that the Nazis even owned the music now.

But not all of it. With a freer hand at rehearsals, the women were able to play music that was not simply propaganda, but that stirred them as musicians. Most, of course, were amateurs, but there were also professionals in their ranks. One was cellist Anita Lasker (see page 61), and another was Fania Fénelon, a French pianist, composer and cabaret singer, both of whom would survive to write memoirs about the orchestra and their life in the camp.

A third was Alma Rosé. She replaced Czajkowska as leader of the orchestra in August 1943. Under Rosé the orchestra grew in numbers – from around 20 members to 47, including five singers – and proficiency. But of course, for every new member there was the possible loss of another – being a member of the orchestra made it less likely you would go to the gas chamber, but no less likely that you would die.

Rosé sometimes grew angry at the amateur players – some of them had simply had music lessons as children and now were desperately trying to remember their scales in order to survive – but there is no doubt that she played a role in making sure that "her girls" were less likely to be exterminated. Ultimately, even the worst playing was tolerated in order to keep the musicians from the chambers.

And when they made music, and when it went well, there is no doubt that at least for a moment they were filled with hope, and the feeling that the tradition would continue. Whatever the Nazis believed, music cannot be owned. But it can be passed along.

Alma Rosé did not survive the camp. She died, aged 37, in mysterious circumstances – a sudden illness, possibly food poisoning. A third conductor, the Ukrainian pianist Sonia Winogradowa, took over, but as Auschwitz began to crumble, so the orchestra started to dwindle, and the players were in fact transported to Bergen-Belsen in November 1944. The orchestra did not play there. But on the day of the liberation of that camp, Fania Fénelon was interviewed by the BBC and sang "La Marseillaise" and "God Save the King", backed by other former members. Music had won.

THE CELLIST OF AUSCHWITZ: PART TWO

Anita Lasker was moved to Bergen-Belsen along with other players in the Women's Orchestra, but not before one of the strangest moments of her life. Perhaps the most notorious Nazi at Auschwitz was Dr Josef Mengele, known for his grotesque medical experiments on inmates, including women and children, especially twins. Few people in history have proved to be so evil, and seemingly without a soul.

And yet one day he stood before Anita and asked her to play for him "Träumerei" by Robert Schumann – known in English as "Scenes from Childhood" – 13 exquisite pieces of music evoking childhood memories. How to reconcile Mengele's crimes with this moment always haunted Anita – this was a man who would greet children from the trains and then take them away and experiment on them until they were dead.

At Bergen-Belsen, inmates survived for six months with almost nothing to eat – the gradual defeat of the Nazis meant even greater food shortages than before, and of course concentration camp inmates were at the end of the queue. But on 15 April 1945 the British Army arrived and Anita and her sister Renate were saved.

With the help of older sister Marianne, they were able to get to England. There Renate became an interpreter with the British Army. And Anita?

Anita not only became one of the world's greatest cellists, but is now part of a musical dynasty – showing that hope cannot be destroyed, even by places like Auschwitz. In 1951 she married Peter Wallfisch, also from Breslau, and himself a concert pianist – Wallfisch had emigrated to England that year. He later became professor of piano at Britain's most prestigious music school, the Royal College of Music.

Their daughter Maya became a psychotherapist, and their son Raphael followed Anita into playing the cello, and also became one of the world's best. He married the Australian Baroque violinist Elizabeth Hunt, and they have three children: Golden-Globe-winning composer of film scores Benjamin Wallfisch; cellist and baritone Simon Wallfisch, who was the main cellist in the Holocaust Memorial Day programme on BBC Two in 2015; and singer-songwriter Joanna Wallfisch.

After nearly 50 years away from Germany, Anita returned there on tour with the English Chamber Orchestra in 1994, and in December 2020, aged 95, she was awarded the Officer's Cross of the Order of Merit of the Federal Republic of Germany. In his speech, the German Ambassador to Britain said, "To this day, you have helped keep the memory of the Holocaust alive for future generations", and expressed Germany's gratitude for this.

THE CELLIST OF AUSCHWITZ: PART TWO

Anita Lasker-Wallfisch is one of the great symbols of hope that Auschwitz has given us. In 2018, she was invited to speak at the German parliament, the Bundestag. She stressed: "There are no excuses and no explanations for what happened all those years ago. All that remains is hope: the hope that ultimately, one day, reason will prevail."

KINDERTRANSPORT

Some of the stories of hope are not set in Auschwitz – they are about those who were spared the terrible fate that so many others suffered, such as people like Edith Goldberg.

It was 1938. As the world gradually became aware of the true horrors of Nazi repression, the persecution of the Jews and eventually the horrors of the concentration camps, many of the Allied nations began programmes to provide any help they could.

Perhaps the most famous of these was Britain's Kindertransport (children's transport), which brought some 10,000 Jewish children to Britain, placed them in foster homes, in hostels and on farms, and gave them schooling. In many cases, these children were the only survivors of the Holocaust in their families.

The programme started in response to the notorious Kristallnacht – the "Night of Broken Glass" on 9–10 November 1938. During that night, Jewish homes, schools and hospitals were attacked by raging mobs, some of them paramilitary, but often simply citizens, while the authorities – Hitler's police and army – watched on or helped. Rioters destroyed over 1,400 synagogues, while 7,000 Jewish businesses were ruined. It is not known how many died, but approximately 30,000 Jewish men were arrested and taken to the concentration camps.

The world – increasingly horrified by the "legal" persecution of Jews – could no longer stand by. In Britain, on 15 November, a delegation of British, Jewish and Quaker leaders appealed to the prime minister, Neville Chamberlain, to intervene. A cabinet meeting was held, and it was announced the next day that the government would waive all immigration requirements for Jewish children under the age of 17. No limit was set for the number of children Britain would take.

Within days a network of organizations had been set up across Europe, while the BBC asked for foster homes – and a day later had 500 offers. And incredibly, on 2 December, less than three weeks after Kristallnacht, the first convoy of 196 children arrived in Harwich in Essex. These were children identified as most at risk – those whose parents had been taken, orphans, and the children of the poor. They could carry only one suitcase, and less than ten marks in money. The vast majority would never see their parents again.

Edith Goldberg was born in Kaiserslautern in southwest Germany. Her father and uncle had been arrested on Kristallnacht and spent three weeks in Dachau before being released – neither would discuss what had happened there, but Edith remembers her father being completely changed.

Edith's mother contacted the Jewish Refugee Committee in England and put forward 11-year-old Edith and her eight-year-old sister Irmgard as potential Kindertransport evacuees, and they were accepted. Their parents took them to the nearest station in Frankfurt – one can barely imagine what Edith's mother and father were thinking as they drove there, or as they drove back. Edith would later recall her mother crying and her father looking stern. She had her doll with her, and a tiny necklace her mother had given her, which she kept well hidden.

They were taken by train to Rotterdam, and then by ferry to Harwich. Two women accompanied them to Leeds, in Northern England, where they were fostered to next-door neighbours – Edith to the Craskins, and Irmgard to the Bloomfields. They both started school three days later, despite not understanding any English. Edith later reflected that her foster family treated her as well as their own three daughters.

Three years later, at 14, she left school – not uncommon for a girl in England at the time – and started working at Schofields, a prestigious department store in Leeds. Soon after, she became a British citizen and met her future husband, Jack. They married in 1951 and started their own business in Leeds. They were married for 62 years, before Edith passed away in 2013, leaving two children and numerous grandchildren.

The fate of her parents and uncle – along with the rest of her wider family – is as to be expected. They were placed in Gurs internment camp in 1940, and then transferred to Auschwitz in 1942. How long they survived there is unknown, but we do know that before they went to that final camp they were able to exchange letters with their daughters and would have known they were safe and happy.

STORIES OF HOPE FROM AUSCHWITZ

Perhaps that gave them some hope, amid all the carnage and horror around them – the hope that their family would endure once all of this was over.

And they did.

MAN'S SEARCH FOR MEANING

According to the Library of Congress, it remains one of the top ten most influential books in the history of the United States. According to its author, the Auschwitz survivor Viktor Frankl, it was written in nine days. *Man's Search for Meaning* may not have provided hope to those who were locked away in the concentration camp, but it has brought hope to many millions who never want the camps to happen again.

Frankl became head of the neurological department at the General Polyclinic Hospital in Vienna after the war, and the book was originally called *A Psychologist Experiences the Concentration Camp*. Frankl was interested in not only his own experiences but those of other inmates – how does one believe that life has any meaning after such an experience?

Born in 1905, Frankl had become fascinated by psychology at a young age and even corresponded with Sigmund Freud as a teenager. He was drawn to neurology, and by the time the war began he was head of neurology at Rothschild Hospital in Vienna – no other hospitals would accept Jews.

STORIES OF HOPE FROM AUSCHWITZ

In 1942, he and his family were sent to the Theresienstadt concentration camp, where his father died of pneumonia. The rest of the family were then taken to Auschwitz, where his mother and three brothers were gassed. His wife Tilly died of typhus soon after. Frankl himself somehow survived, and would spend the rest of his life grappling with the question – does life have a meaning? Did his?

The book closely examines the reactions of the inmates in the face of torture, death, loss, starvation and the loss of hope. What the Nazis were doing was dehumanizing the inmates, which raises the question: what is it to be human? Is it just to be a sentient being, or is there more to it than that?

Frankl was forcefully struck by the words of the German philosopher Friedrich Nietzsche – "He who has a 'why' to live for can bear almost any 'how'." Someone who has lost their reason to live – be it their family, their religion, friendships or work, for example – will lose their sense of reason, and the smallest difficulty can become enormous. But the opposite is also true – someone who has a reason to live can endure great suffering and still retain their sense of humanity. As Frankl put it, "In some ways suffering ceases to be suffering at the moment it finds a meaning."

For many survivors, this meant telling their stories, giving them a form, helping in the battle to stop anything like this happening again. It was a battle that Frankl actively took part in. Having lost so many of his family, he needed a higher purpose – to continue to work against fascism, and to help all those who were struggling to live meaningful lives. In his work as a psychiatrist, Frankl helped thousands of people across life's spectrum, making the idea of "meaning" central to mental health. His daughter and grandson have followed him into the family trade.

In *Man's Search for Meaning* he wrote that the one thing that couldn't be taken away was how he chose to respond to what was done to him. "The last of one's freedoms is to choose one's attitude in any given circumstance." His words still resonate today.

THE CONFIDANTE

When Auschwitz was liberated, the hunt began for those who had staffed the camp but were no longer present. Allied investigators swept across Europe looking for the perpetrators of one of the worst ever crimes against humanity.

On 1 May 1945, they arrested a woman named Maria Stromberger at her home in Bregenz in Austria. She had been a nurse in Auschwitz from October 1942 to January 1945, when she had been released due to an inflammation of the blood vessels and a diagnosis of morphine addiction.

At Auschwitz she had served under Dr Eduard Wirths, and Allied investigators were ready to charge her for her crimes. But as they sifted through the evidence and spoke to those who had survived the camp, a different and astonishing story emerged. Stromberger had worked for the anti-Nazi resistance, and the reason she was in Auschwitz was to try and alleviate the suffering of the prisoners. During her time there, Stromberger smuggled weapons, food, medicine and information to Auschwitz inmates, and delivered information about the camp and its prisoners to the public.

STORIES OF HOPE FROM AUSCHWITZ

Born a Catholic in Austria in 1898, Stromberger moved between various jobs, before finally beginning to study nursing – her dream job since childhood – at the age of 39. Graduating in 1940, after the war had begun, her first job was to tend to German soldiers repatriated from the battlefield. It was from them that she started to hear stories about what was happening in the concentration camps.

She requested a transfer to Poland, and there she encountered a number of patients from Auschwitz who had become infected with typhus, one of the main causes of death in the camp. Their distress and physical injuries moved Stromberger. She made a momentous decision – she would go to the camp and try to help. She requested, and was granted, a transfer.

She would later describe the initial horror of the camp – typhus was everywhere, and from her office she could hear the screams of inmates as they were being led to the gas chambers. She fainted when she saw one man throw himself against an electric fence and die. She herself had to request sick leave, unable to bear the sight of the emaciated inmates. But Maria Stromberger steeled herself and returned.

Not allowed to treat inmates herself – this was exclusively the job of physicians, under the supervision of Dr Eduard Wirths – she gradually came to become a confidante of a prisoner named Edek Pys. They worked together to smuggle food meant for SS officers to the prisoners, and to enable her to visit sick inmates at times when they were unsupervised. When Pys himself fell ill with typhus, she not only tended to him but surreptitiously carried out some of his work detail.

THE CONFIDANTE

She also joined the resistance movement within the camp and, with her ability to move around the entire complex, became a key individual in transmitting plans across Auschwitz. Also, the fact that she was able to leave the camp enabled her to collect information for the inmates and acquire rations, pistols, ammunition and explosives.

But the help she provided was also medical. As well as tending to the sick, she worked on those around her, particularly Dr Wirths, to make them change the way they treated the inmates – including helping to push for the immunization of prisoners from typhus, something that Hermann Langbein (see page 19) estimated saved 93,000 lives.

On several occasions, suspicions were raised against Stromberger, usually to do with the way she related to prisoners, and Wirths was known to have warned her she might end up interred herself, but he also defended her against all accusations – apart from anything else, he did not want to lose his best nurse.

Perhaps her most audacious move was to hold Christmas parties for the inmates in 1943 and 1944, smuggling in food and champagne. While the number who could be there was small – Langbein was one of 17 who attended in 1943, and among them were Jews and communists who did not usually celebrate Christmas – it gave a signal of hope, even to those who did not attend.

In 1944, as the number of killings increased, Stromberger was ordered, with all medical staff, to sign a document agreeing to facilitate the deaths. She refused. Wirths allowed her to deface that part of the document, as to leave it empty would have seen her become one of the prisoners, but for the first time she thought of fleeing the camp. She stayed.

When she became ill in December of that year – ground down by work, stress and distress, Wirths prescribed morphine, which she surreptitiously tipped out or gave to suffering inmates. It was, however, a painkiller she could have used – eventually she was sent to a neurological clinic in Prague to recuperate. Wirths "misdiagnosed" a morphine addiction. It was his way of helping her get away from the camp as the Allies closed in.

When she was arrested and her plight became known, huge numbers of survivors, including Pys, came forward to vouch for her and provide evidence of her work for the resistance. The Polish newspaper *Echo Krakowa* ran a front-page story calling for her release – its new editor, Tadeusz Hołuj, was a survivor himself. On 23 September 1946, she was released after six months in prison, and she was later not only completely exonerated but received a large number of honours from Holocaust organizations.

But she had no interest in becoming in any way political and refused to attend reunions of survivors, feeling that her presence there was inappropriate. It may be, though, that her final act on her deathbed in 1957 was another gesture of solidarity with all of those who had burned in the fires of Auschwitz. Although it is forbidden by Catholicism, she asked to be cremated.

THE COUGH

They were two brilliant composers. Karel Ančerl was born in 1908 into a prosperous Jewish family in the village of Tučapy in southern Bohemia, now part of the Czech Republic. He studied composition and conducting at the Prague Conservatory between 1925 and 1929, along with chamber music, violin and percussion. He found fame conducting avant-garde music with the orchestra of the theatre Osvobozené divadlo in Prague.

Pavel Haas was born in 1899 in Brno, in what is now the Czech Republic, into a Moravian-Jewish family. After proving to be a piano prodigy, he started formal musical training at the Brno conservatory at the age of 14, under perhaps the Czech Republic's greatest twentieth-century composer, Leoš Janáček. Haas's first opera, *Šarlatán* (*The Charlatan*), was first performed in Brno to a rapturous reception in April 1938.

Both Ančerl and Haas seemed assured of glittering careers. And then the Nazis invaded and defeated Czechoslovakia. The pair were no longer famous musicians first and foremost. First and foremost, they were Jews.

STORIES OF HOPE FROM AUSCHWITZ

They were sent to Theresienstadt concentration camp; Haas in 1941 and Ančerl in 1942. Haas had divorced his beloved wife Soňa in 1938, in order that she and their daughter Olga would be spared the fate of Czech Jews. He also tried to get the family away to the US, but permission came too late. In the camp, he suffered from terrible depression, and it was another composer, Gideon Klein, who managed to coax him into writing music while he was there.

Meanwhile Ančerl became the leader of the large Terezín String Orchestra and started to organize cultural and music life there. In part, this involved having to conduct music for Nazi propaganda films – Theresienstadt was the camp where the regime used to pretend that the concentration camps were internment facilities.

This included a film called *Theresienstadt*, in which Ančerl conducted the orchestra for one of Haas's works. Flowerpots hid the fact that many of the orchestra were barefoot; loose clothing covered the fact that they were starving.

Ančerl also conducted another work by Haas, his *Study for String Orchestra*, which remains the most famous piece by the composer. After the war it would be reconstructed by those who had participated in the performance and survived.

Though the film *Theresienstadt* may have served its purpose for the Nazis, it did not help any of the participants. All those who had been involved in the film were herded into cattle trucks for the final transport to Auschwitz on 15 October 1944. This included a number of children who had performed in a children's opera called *Brundibár*, written by fellow inmate Hans Krása. It also included Karel Ančerl and Pavel Haas. Ančerl's wife, Valy, and son Jan – who had been

THE COUGH

born in Theresienstadt – were also on that transport. Both were murdered on arrival.

The composers Hans Krása and Gideon Klein would not survive Auschwitz. But what happened to Karel Ančerl and Pavel Haas is remarkable. According to the testimony of Karel Ančerl, Haas stood next to him after their arrival at Auschwitz. Josef Mengele was about to send Ančerl to the gas chamber first. But at that moment Haas dissolved in a coughing fit, which Ančerl was sure he put on. Mengele decided to send the weaker man to the gas chamber, and Haas was taken away and killed.

Ančerl survived. After the liberation of Auschwitz, he made it home, and from 1946 to 1947 he was a conductor for the State Opera of Prague. He would become acknowledged as one of the world's great conductors, conducting the Toronto Symphony Orchestra from 1968 until his death in Toronto in 1973.

History is a strange thing – so many small decisions can lead to monumental decisions. Why did Pavel Haas pretend to have a coughing fit, knowing it would lead to his death? Did he believe the life of Karel Ančerl was worth more than his own? Whatever happened at that moment, in that spilt-second decision, we can take away one thing from it – that Pavel Haas was full of hope, for a world where the survival of Karel Ančerl was important.

CHOICELESS CHOICES

"*Hashem*" – it means "The Name" but is also one of the ways in Judaism to refer to God. And, in 2024, Bronia Brandman told the *Mishpacha Jewish Family Weekly*: "*Hashem* has saved my life seven times". An Auschwitz survivor, she has been on a journey that took her from a small village in Poland to the White House, where she talked with President Joe Biden on Holocaust Remembrance Day. "Today she shared her story – and spoke for millions who never had a chance," Biden said afterwards.

It is a journey that has involved her witnessing some of the most horrifying human behaviour in history, but all the time she has had faith that *Hashem* was there.

Bronia Brandman was born Bronia Rubin in Jaworzno, Poland, one of six children of a hardware store owner Irael Rubin and his wife Ida. She had three older siblings (Mila, Mendek and Tulek) and two younger sisters (Rutka and Macia).

When the Nazis invaded in 1939, the family fled to another town called Mielec but that was immediately under siege. She managed to avoid a German soldier by hiding behind a door. That night was the first time, she says, that *Hashem* saved her. The family decided to return to their hometown.

In March 1942, the order was given for the oldest child of each family to report for deportation. Mendek volunteered to go in place of his older sister, Mila, and was taken to Blechhammer labour camp. The following year the rest of the family was herded into a school yard and surrounded by Germans with guns and dogs. Urged to leave by her mother, she later said that she just walked out. Her life had been saved a second time – her parents and brother, Tulek, were deported to Auschwitz and murdered.

But a year later there was no escape. Having fled to a nearby town, Sosnowiec, the four sisters were captured and deported to Auschwitz. Dr Mengele, as always, was waiting there to inspect the children and select those who would go to the gas chamber. The oldest sister Mila was directed to the right to be saved, while Bronia and her two younger sisters were directed to the left.

That was when Bronia made the first of what she was to come to identify as a "choiceless choice". This term was coined by Lawrence Langer in his 1982 book *Versions of Survival: The Holocaust and the Human Spirit*, to describe the no-win situations faced by Jews during the Holocaust. These were the sort of choices in which there was no option that did not cause trauma, and are a major cause of survivor guilt.

She started to go to the left as ordered but then suddenly ran across to her adored older sister Mila, even as her other sisters were sent to the gas chamber. This was the third

CHOICELESS CHOICES

time, she says, that *Hashem* saved her life, but the first time she was left with complicated feelings of guilt. Of course, had she gone left, she would not have been able to save her sisters anyway, and she would have died, and yet to abandon them...

It was not long before she made another choiceless choice, and one that remains a major trauma in her life. Her adored Mila came down with typhus and was sent to the medical facility. Not wanting to be parted from her sister, Bronia went too. By then the girls had met a woman named Bozenka Teichnerova, a Jewish nurse from Slovakia who worked in the Auschwitz infirmary. She helped hide Bronia in the infirmary with her sister.

But then Bozenka found out that the infirmary was to be "cleared" – everyone there was to be sent to the gas chamber. She told Bronia. She faced an impossible choice: should she stay with Mila, who was dying, and perish with her? Or leave and save herself?

She left. Mila was sent to the gas chambers with the rest of the sick. Again, nothing would have changed had she gone with Mila. But the psychological effects of Bronia's choice were devastating.

There was one more amazing event to go. Alone in the camp, Bronia fell victim to typhus and ended up in the same infirmary. And again it was decided to clear everyone out. And again Bozenka risked her life by telling Bronia.

That same day, Mengele came to the barracks and wrote down everyone's number. "Bozenka pushed me to beg him for my life," Bronia remembers. "Naturally, I hesitated, but Bozenka kept insisting."

Remarkably, Bronia did just that – she approached Mengele and asked to be spared. At that moment a siren sounded, to warn of an air raid. Mengele ran for cover and Bronia ran back to bed. Later, Mengele's junior officer asked Bozenka how Mengele had responded to Bronia. She lied that Mengele agreed to remove Bronia's card, as well as the cards of five other prisoners, from the gas chamber list. Bronia believes this was the fifth time *Hashem* saved her life.

Hashem – and Bozenka – would save Bronia one more time. Having suffered a second bout of typhus in December 1944, which left her in a coma for four weeks, Bronia woke just before the camp was evacuated and had to start on a death march. Still weak from her bout of typhus, Bronia was struggling to stand and saw an SS guard preparing to shoot. But Bozenka continued to look after the women on the march, and she grabbed Bronia, hauling her away from the bullets. She had evaded death for a sixth time.

Once installed at Ravensbrück, Bozenka carried out her final act of courage, sneaking 13-year-old Bronia in with a group of adults who were being transported elsewhere. It would later transpire that all the children who remained were gassed. Bronia had evaded death for a seventh time.

Her final internment was in the Neustadt-Glewe camp, where aircraft parts were being made, and which was liberated by the Red Army on 2 May 1945. The war had ended. But there was another miracle or two in store. Bronia's brother, Mendek, had also survived – the only one of 40 men taken from their village who had. And so had Bozenka, who Bronia met again after the war.

CHOICELESS CHOICES

When a cousin in America secured visas for both Bronia and Mendek, Bronia had to say goodbye to her saviour. Astonishingly, she was still only 15 years old.

Bozenka met Bronia's family, including her children and grandchildren, when they visited her in Slovakia. Bozenka lived a full life, passing away at 96.

In the US, Bronia had to confront her trauma. She married and had children but spent her time, she said, preparing them for the next Holocaust. She believes that if it happened once, it could happen again, however civilized we all seem to be. Unable to cry, even on the death of her husband, she says that it also took 25 years for her to be able to laugh. She would later say that while she trusts individuals, she does not trust humanity. The crimes of the Nazis, she said, are not theoretical. They happened to her.

But she gradually came to realize that, in her words, a child only grows stronger through love. It was not until she was 65 that she began to share her experiences with others, and to look for the positives in life. This was part of her victory over Nazism.

It is a message she has shared many times since, including when she was asked to speak to the families of those who survived the 2012 mass shooting at Sandy Hook Elementary School that left 26 dead. One survivor wrote to her that "your story of resilience in the Holocaust has helped me to open up about my experiences". If trauma can work down the generations, then so can healing.

Bronia Brandman, with help from Bozenka Teichnerova, and from *Hashem*, has helped to heal many people, including herself. And every time she does so, it is another victory against the Nazis who tried so hard to kill her and her people. As Joe Biden wrote to her after their meeting, "It was my greatest honour to meet with you. You have so much to be proud of!"

NATIONAL HERO

In a way, every survival story from Auschwitz is one of hope. Many of those who came out alive went on to live fulfilling lives, and of course produce families – exactly what Adolf Hitler and his minions didn't want. Every child who is descended from an Auschwitz survivor is a victory against attempted genocide.

But some survivors have also made an even bigger contribution to the world – and few have contributed as much as Simone Veil, one of France's greatest fighters for women's rights and for a Europe that would work together, rather than one always balanced on the precipice of war. For her work, she was awarded France's highest award, the Grand Cross of the Légion d'honneur, and was made an honorary dame of the United Kingdom, an incredibly rare honour.

Veil was born Simone Jacob on 13 July 1927 to a Jewish family in Nice, the daughter of a well-respected and award-winning architect. Her mother was a chemistry student who gave up her studies to raise her four children, of whom Simone was the youngest. Her parents were atheists, but remained proud of their Jewishness.

Their atheism didn't matter, however, once France had surrendered to Germany in 1940. Being a Jew was, notoriously, a racial designation, not a religious or cultural one. The family was as vulnerable as those who practised the faith. Simone and her siblings were banned from school, her father was banned from work.

The family split up, living with other people under assumed names. Simone's older sister Denise left to join the resistance, while Simone home-schooled herself and managed to graduate in March 1944. It would be her last day of freedom for some time. The next day as she went to celebrate her graduation with friends, she was arrested, as were the rest of her family.

On 7 April 1944, Simone, her mother and her sister Madeleine were sent first to Drancy, a transit camp, and then six days later to Auschwitz. She would later find out that her sister Denise, working for the resistance, had also been captured, and went on to spend the rest of the war in Ravensbrück concentration camp, built exclusively for women, where of the 132,000 women who passed through, 50,000 died. When the camp was evacuated in April 1945, there were only 3,500 survivors – including Denise.

The fate of Denise was not known by Simone at the time, nor was that of her father or brother Jean. They were sent to the Baltic states and never heard of again. One can imagine their fate.

Simone would spend a year in Auschwitz, seeing others who had been incarcerated led to the gas chambers, and witnessing the violence meted out to men, women and children by the camp guards. As the tide of war turned

NATIONAL HERO

against Germany, many of these guards became ever more desperate and sadistic. How did she find hope in this hell?

For Simone, as she was to show in later life, it was in the idea that humans were more dignified than this, and that this dignity is not a given but needs to be fought for at every opportunity. As she put it many years later when talking about Auschwitz, "It's here, where absolute evil was perpetrated, that the will must resurface for a fraternal world, a world based on respect of man and his dignity."

But that was in the future. In January 1945, Simone, along with her mother and sister, were sent on a march to Bergen-Belsen concentration camp, some 800 kilometres (500 miles) away, where her mother died of typhus. Her sister Madeleine also fell ill, but fortunately she was still alive when the camp was liberated in April 1945.

Simone returned to France and began studying law in Paris, where she met and married Antoine Veil. She graduated as a magistrate, and in 1956 began to work for the French Ministry of Justice, where one of her first tasks was to improve the conditions for women in prison – no doubt influenced by her own time as an inmate.

It was the beginning of a working life spent advocating for women's rights, including helping to achieve the right to dual parental control of family legal matters, control that had until then been the preserve of men.

Simone Veil was Minister of Health from 1974 to 1979, and is best known for two laws that are regarded in France as landmarks in women's rights – the 1974 law giving access to the contraceptive pill, and the 1975 law legalizing abortion.

STORIES OF HOPE FROM AUSCHWITZ

But there was one lesson from Auschwitz that fired her later political career. World War Two had come just 21 years after the end of the first. Europe could not keep doing this to itself. Simone became a passionate advocate of European cooperation, spending 1979 to 1994 as a member of the European parliament. When she died in 2017, aged 89, 72 years had passed since World War Two, a period of peace in Western Europe unheard of for centuries.

On her death, she received a national ceremony and military honours, and was buried beside Antoine, who had died in 2013. Five years later she was reburied in the Pantheon, one of only 81 French citizens accorded that honour. Could she have hoped for even a part of that life as she awaited her fate in Auschwitz?

In his eulogy, French president Emmanuel Macron said France was a better nation because of Veil. "You shined your light into our lives," he said, "a light that no one could extinguish." Not even Auschwitz.

IN THE COMMANDANT'S HOUSE

It was a painting that condemned him to going to Auschwitz, and it was through painting that he managed to escape – not physically, but mentally and emotionally. It was also painting that saw Mieczyslaw Koscielniak experience one of the strangest episodes in the history of Auschwitz.

Born on 29 January 1912, Mieczyslaw Koscielniak was always an artist. As a child he drew incessantly, but then so did his older brother Tadeusz (born 1910) and younger brother Władysław (born 1916) – all three were to become renowned artists in Poland. Tadeusz is best known for his religious paintings, Władysław for his photography and graphic design in books – and Mieczyslaw for chronicling the horrors of Auschwitz.

In 1928, 16-year-old Mieczyslaw painted a picture expressing the rage many Poles felt about German domination and threats against their country – it depicted Germans being shot by Poles during World War One. It was one of a great many pictures the young man created, and it is possible he had forgotten about it by 1939, when the

Nazis invaded. But it turned out the Germans had not – they tracked the artist down and arrested him on 6 March 1941. He was sent to Auschwitz, arriving on 2 May 1941 with 208 other men. The camp was not yet fully operational – the sewage system was still being put in – but the air of terror that was to reign over it was already there. As soon as the men left the train, they were attacked by guards with dogs and beaten with sticks. Compared to what else would happen at Auschwitz this may seem mild, but we must always remind ourselves that even some of the lesser horrors of Auschwitz were already way beyond what is generally considered acceptable, even in war.

Koscielniak estimated that when he arrived there were only about 15–16,000 prisoners, borne out by his prisoner number, 15261. He was assigned work to help build the camp. Already it was clear that Auschwitz needed to increase in size to accommodate all the prisoners – the main camp, where Koscielniak arrived, would eventually swell to 40 camps, a massive prison complex. In his testimony after the war, Koscielniak said that building in Birkenau started in the summer of 1941 and that in the autumn 12,000 Soviet prisoners were forced to work – according to some records, after a few months only 56 of them remained alive.

He himself worked on building the factories for Buna-Werke, a chemical company specializing in the production of polymer materials such as plastics and artificial rubber for the Nazis.

At the time, there were few Jewish prisoners arriving and those who did were directed to the factories. It was common knowledge that a Jew didn't stay at the camp for longer

IN THE COMMANDANT'S HOUSE

than two weeks. In 1942 and 1943, Jewish transports became large in number – they were arriving from France, Belgium, Holland, Germany and Czechoslovakia. This was all overseen by the camp commandant, Rudolf Höss.

Höss was the longest-serving commandant of Auschwitz Concentration Camp (from 4 May 1940 to November 1943, and again from 8 May 1944 to 18 January 1945). Born in 1901 in a strict Catholic family, he claimed to have been briefly abducted by Romanies as a child, which started his descent into racism. His father, a coffee merchant, intended him for the priesthood, and he brought his son up on strict religious principles and with military discipline.

In his teens Höss turned away from religion, and when his father died he began moving towards a military life. When World War One started in 1914, he lied about his age and worked in a military hospital before joining the army; at 17 he was the youngest non-commissioned officer. He was wounded three times and awarded the Iron Cross for bravery – the same honour Adolf Hitler was to receive in that war.

Höss joined the Nazi Party in 1922 (member number 3240) and renounced his affiliation with the Catholic Church. In 1924 he and Hitler's future private secretary beat a schoolteacher to death and received ten-year sentences, although he only served four years. In 1934 he joined the SS. At the start of the war, he was assigned leadership of the Sachsenhausen concentration camp. On 18 January he made a group of prisoners stand outside in temperatures of −26°C (−15°F), leading to 145 deaths in one night. He was seen as ideal for running the new camp at Auschwitz.

Stories of his brutality and sadism are endless, but perhaps it is enough to say he was not only a willing but an enthusiastic leader in the Nazi experiments in mass murder. It was he who instituted the selection of prisoners for work or for gassing, and he who perfected the use of Zyklon B in the chambers.

Mass murder, he later wrote, was not that difficult – you could, he noted, "kill 2,000 people in half an hour". According to Höss, it was the burning that took all the time.

Meanwhile, Koscielniak continued to work on the building site. One day a guard there found out that he was a painter – of course he was at the camp for exactly that, but he was no longer a name but a number, so it was not common knowledge – and taunted him, saying he couldn't believe such a hopeless man could be any such thing. Koscielniak replied that he could draw a picture in 5 minutes that would show that he was indeed an artist or else the guard could have him whipped. The guard gave him a pencil and paper, and Koscielniak produced a sketch of the guard that impressed him immensely. The man who had painted Germans being shot by Poles was now to be used by the Nazis as a propaganda painter.

He was assigned to do various art chores on top of his slave labour, such as producing posters and painting pictures of the camp orchestra, and he was also requested by many of the SS to paint their portraits. This gave Koscielniak access to art materials, and he was able to smuggle out extra paper and pencils. He started recording daily life at the camp.

Koscielniak's drawings are one of the most powerful records we have of life in Auschwitz – some 300 survived

IN THE COMMANDANT'S HOUSE

and are on display in the Auschwitz-Birkenau State Museum. They show the struggles, the brutality, they show death. But they also show moments of beauty and fellow feeling, inmates working together, giving what support they can. They show moments of hope, and the drawings, by showing that the Nazis could not kill human creativity, *are* moments of hope in themselves.

Koscielniak was asked by camp commandant Rudolf Höss to evaluate paintings that had been confiscated from the Poles who had owned the property where Auschwitz was built. In order to do so, Koscielniak was brought to the house Höss lived in on site and stayed there for three days, going through the paintings, advising him which were good and how best to display them. While he was guarded at all times, this meant that Koscielniak, in what must have been an incredibly disconcerting time, was able to sleep in a proper bed and use hot water and soap. After the three days, he was sent back out into the camp, and those three days ended up seeming like a dream.

He continued to see moments of awful brutality, which he related in his testimony after the war. In his descriptions he talked of inmates being beaten with sticks, and some who were chosen at random to have chains placed around their waists and attached to a well bucket, which was lowered to tighten the chain until the prisoner passed out.

He also described the long days of brutal hard work that began at 4 a.m. in the summer and 4.30 a.m. in the winter, and didn't end until 5.30 p.m., after which there was a roll call which might last until after midnight. If the prisoners were lucky, and no one was missing, they would then get thin soup as their meal.

In 1942 Koscielniak was reassigned to work in a warehouse, unloading trains at the sidings. Two hundred to three hundred prisoners, divided into sections, worked at the warehouses, nearly all of them Polish or Jewish. The cargo was often Zyklon B for the gas chambers.

He came down with typhus, as so many did in the unsanitary conditions of the camp. Often those with typhus were simply beaten to death and he waited for the same to happen to him, but he was fortunate enough to escape this fate.

Then in January 1945 – Koscielniak was one of the longest serving Auschwitz inmates – the liberation began. As the inmates left, the weaker ones, mostly women, were shot on their way out.

For Koscielniak it was not the end of the horror – he was sent to Mauthausen where he endured another four months of hell, before finally being freed in May 1945 from Ebensee Concentration Camp in Austria, where he had been taken in the dying days of the war. In a strange irony, when the US liberators, led by Colonel James H. Polk, commander of the 3rd Cavalry Group, found out he was an artist, they too asked him to paint their portraits. The one he did of Polk is now held by the colonel's family.

Koscielniak stayed with the US Army for six months and the overall commander, General Patton, offered to enable him to emigrate to the United States. Koscielniak refused. He was Polish, he had suffered as a Pole, and he wanted

IN THE COMMANDANT'S HOUSE

to take part in remaking the Polish society that Hitler had tried, and failed, to destroy.

After the war, Koscielniak returned to Warsaw, then to Ustka in 1979 and finally, in 1989, to Słupsk. He became a member of the Société européenne de culture (SEC) and was awarded the National Education Committee Medal and the Gold Cross of Merit – each award a victory against the Nazis. He continued to paint, but it is those 300 drawings created in Auschwitz-Birkenau that define his legacy and of which he remained most proud.

Rudolf Höss fled Auschwitz at the end of the war and pretended to be a gardener named Franz Lang. He was arrested in 1946. On 25 May 1946, Höss was handed over to Polish authorities and charged with war crimes. The trial lasted from 11 to 29 March 1947 and he was sentenced to death by hanging on 2 April. Shortly before his execution, Höss returned to the Catholic Church. Having written an autobiography while in prison, denying any responsibility for anything that happened in Auschwitz, he penned a short note confessing his crimes, which was found after his death. On 16 April 1947, Höss was hanged. At the request of former camp prisoners, the execution was carried out in Auschwitz. His body was burned and the ashes were disposed of.

Koscielniak outlived Höss by nearly 50 years, dying in 1993, and was buried in a hero's grave.

THE DIARY

Born in 1889 to a German Jewish family, Otto Frank studied economics from 1908 to 1909 before spending two years in New York, training in business. He returned to Germany in 1911, aged 22, and was drafted in 1915 to the Imperial German Army. Promoted twice, he received the Iron Cross for bravery and identified as a German patriot.

When World War One was over, he started a career in banking, and in 1925, aged 36, he married Edith Holländer – an heiress to a scrap-metal and industrial-supply business. He was a man of some standing, comfortably off. The couple had two daughters and life seemed safe and secure.

Then, in 1933, the Nazis came to power. Being in a position to do so, Frank decided to evacuate with his family, first to Aachen, his wife's hometown, and then on to Amsterdam, where his brother-in-law helped him find work in a jam-making factory. Edith's mother joined them. But the Nazis invaded the Netherlands in 1940, and in 1942, when the systematic deportation of Jews from the Netherlands began, Frank took his wife, daughters, then aged 16 and 13, and mother-in-law into hiding. The family would spend two years in an attic, relying on the kindness of strangers to keep them safe.

In August 1944 they were discovered – it is not known whether by chance, or if there was an informant. They were all sent to the Dutch transit camp of Westerbork, and soon after placed in the cattle cars that meant transportation to Auschwitz.

Frank was separated from his wife, mother-in-law and daughters. He would spend the next year swinging between hope and despair – were they somewhere else in the camp? Had they been taken somewhere else? He, despite being in his 50s, continued to work. He could only hope that his family was doing the same.

They weren't. His wife and daughters had, it seems, been moved to Bergen-Belsen and died of typhus. Unaware of this, when Westerbork was liberated in January 1945, Frank still held out some hope. He returned to the Netherlands and spent six months searching for his family. By the end of 1945, he realized he was the sole survivor.

But there was something else left behind. His youngest daughter had kept a diary of their time, hidden away, which she had left at the apartment where they hid. Frank typed it up for himself, but then others suggested he try to get it published, as it showed what life had really been like under the Nazis. He did, and *The Diary of a Young Girl* – commonly called *The Diary of Anne Frank* – is now one of the most read books in the world, translated into 70 languages and having sold over 30 million copies. The line, "In spite of everything, I still believe that people are really good at heart," continues to resonate.

THE DIARY

In 1953, Otto Frank married a fellow Auschwitz survivor, Elfriede Geiringer, and in 1960 they established the Anne Frank House in Amsterdam, which to this day commemorates the 13-year-old diarist and reminds us not to forget.

As Anne wrote, "How wonderful it is that nobody need wait a single moment before starting to improve the world."

LOVE IT WAS NOT

It sounds like a movie plot, although a far-fetched one – the story of an SS guard at Auschwitz who falls in love with a Jewish inmate, protects her, saves her sister from the gas chamber and then seeks her out after the war so that, as he put it in his letters to her, they can "be together and keep the many promises we made each other". If it were a movie made in Hollywood, they would meet each other again, renew their promises and end up together, a triumph of love, and, yes, hope.

But this is not Hollywood. And as ever with Auschwitz, things are much more complicated than that. When Helena Citrónová and Nazi SS Lance Corporal Franz Wunsch saw each other again in 1972, she was in the witness box, and he was in court on charges of crimes against humanity.

Citrónová arrived at Auschwitz as part of the first mass transport of 997 Slovak Jewish girls and unmarried young women on 26 March 1942. She was 19 years old and had been born in the Czechoslovakian town of Humenné to a middle-class Hungarian-Jewish family, one of four children. Her older sister, Rozinka (Róza), had left Czechoslovakia when she married, but she returned in 1939 with her four-year-old daughter and her husband when he was unable to find work elsewhere.

This first mass transportation had in fact been organized by the Slovak government, which had sold the women to Nazi Germany for 500 Reichsmarks per person to use as slave labour.

Like the other women, Helena Citrónová had been tricked by the promise of lucrative work abroad and had voluntarily taken the trip. On arrival, they were quickly to find out that the promise was in fact a lie. Citrónová was fit and strong, and she was initially given work helping to demolish a ruined building in the camp. It was a death trap, as new parts of the building fell even as they were clearing away the older parts. "We weren't allowed to run, so when the wall came down, the first girls were crushed and died on the spot," she later described.

After this she got a job in what were known as the Kanada warehouses, where possessions stolen from inmates were sorted, held and distributed. The name Kanada (Canada in German) started as a joke among the prisoners – Canada was regarded as "the Land of Plenty" and the warehouses were full of valuables – and it was soon adopted by the guards.

Citrónová was said by those who knew her to be "flamboyant and full of life" – in one photograph she is shown in her prison outfit smiling vivaciously, perhaps the only photograph ever taken of an Auschwitz inmate smiling at the camera.

She was also known to be a good singer, and in September 1942, on her first day at the warehouse, she was ordered to sing at the birthday party of one of the guards. If she did a good job, she was told, she could stay working at the warehouse; if not, she might be sent back to hard manual labour.

Not knowing any German, she sang the one German language song she knew – "*Liebe war es nie*", "Love it was not". She sang, she said later, with tears running down her face, not because of the lyrics, but because she genuinely thought that if she did a bad job she would be gassed – and so this would be the last time she ever sang. Little was she to know that this moment would change her life forever.

There was one other person in tears. A 20-year-old guard named Franz Wunsch, who was one of the men in charge of the gas chambers, as well as being a manager of the Kanada warehouse, was also at the party. The song may have said "love it was not", but for Wunsch, love it was, and at first sight. Whatever else might be said about him, and about them, there is no doubt that the SS guard was completely swept away by Citrónová.

Intimate and sexual relationships between guards and inmates were, of course, not completely unimaginable, but, unless there are other stories still to be told, these sexual relationships were exclusively non-consensual. A male SS guard was more or less in a position to do as he wanted. Investigations into sexual violence within the camps are still ongoing, but it was certainly present.

What many noted about Wunsch's immediate reaction to Citrónová, and his subsequent behaviour towards her, was that it never went in this direction. Wunsch adored her. After she finished singing, he asked her if she could sing the song again – please. "Suddenly I hear the voice of a human being," she later recalled, "not the roar of animals."

The next day he wrote her a letter, telling her that he loved her. She destroyed that letter, but they kept coming. She said she couldn't even imagine looking at him, feeling nothing but hatred.

But he persisted. He gave her extra food, extra blankets and kept writing the letters – love to a point of madness, Helena later called it. Gradually she started to soften towards him and return some of his affections, although whether there was physical intimacy has never been proved.

Of course, their relationship put both parties at grave risk. For him, colluding in any way with a Jewish inmate, let alone falling in love with one, could have been a death sentence. Apart from anything else, the Nazis had been taught that the Jews were an inferior race, no better, and perhaps worse, than animals. How could one fall in love with them?

And for a Jewish woman, proof that the Nazis were animals, or perhaps worse, was there every day, in the brutality, in the smoke coming out of the chimneys. After the war, women in France who had affairs with German soldiers – "horizontal collaboration" as it was called – were punished by ritual head-shaving as a public form of humiliation. But in the camp, in Auschwitz? Even though Citrónová shared her extra rations with other inmates, she found herself in a very dangerous position – everyone was jealous of her.

Then, in October 1944, Citrónová's sister Róza, along with her husband and two children – a nine-year-old girl and newborn baby boy – were brought to Auschwitz.

LOVE IT WAS NOT

Hearing the news, Helena ran to the gas chamber and pleaded with the SS guards to spare their lives; when they refused, Helena begged them to kill her too.

One of the guards on duty was Franz Wunsch. He ran up to Citrónová, grabbed her and pretended to hit her. As he did so, he whispered to her to give him her sister's name. She told him it was Róza and also told him the names of the children. The children could not be saved, he told her – there was no place for children at Auschwitz. But he did save Róza. For this, Helena would say, she started to love him.

So, who was the man she loved?

Franz Wunsch was born in Drasenhofen in Lower Austria on 21 March 1922 and came to Auschwitz as an SS storm trooper at the age of just 20. He had his first experience of the concentration camp system during a short spell of service at the Dachau concentration camp.

At Auschwitz he was tasked with running Kanada, but he was also a commando leader of the leather factory and was directly involved in managing deaths in the gas chambers. He took part in the selection process, helped load the weak onto trucks and was even prepared to get them into the chambers by use of force – in fact, later testimony about him would describe him as one of the most brutal of the guards.

It is said that after he fell in love with Helena Citrónová he became less brutal – could it be that his idea of Jews was being modified? There are reports that she actually saw him beating an inmate on more than one occasion and made him stop, but this is unconfirmed.

It was Wunsch who took the photograph of Citrónová smiling. Not only that, he made copies of the photo and then cut around her image and placed it on pictures of various locations, to imagine she was somewhere other than Auschwitz. Unable – or unwilling – to help her escape in real life, he had her escape in his fantasies.

It was this bespoke version of Photoshop that inspired the Israeli director Maya Sarfaty when she made a documentary about the relationship, named, of course, *Love It Was Not*. Citrónová's image is moved from setting to setting to tell the story – including the recreation of the trial of Franz Wunsch.

Because, for all of Wunsch's efforts, that would be the only time after the war he would see her. When the camps were liberated, Helena and her Róza headed back to Slovakia – in warm fur-lined boots Wunsch had given them for the journey, along with a final note saying, "I loved you very much." But his love obviously wasn't in the past tense. For much of the next 20 years he tried to track Citrónová down.

Back in Slovakia, the sisters found that everyone they knew was dead and received confirmation that their parents had died in the gas chambers, and their brother had committed suicide during a failed escape attempt. With no reason to stay, they emigrated to what was then called Palestine.

Wunsch meanwhile had been arrested by the SS, but he was only charged with stealing a few small items – leather gloves, cigarettes, a hunting knife and a torch – despite all that had gone missing from the Kanada stores. He spent five weeks in solitary confinement in a Nazi jail, and was then released back into civilian life. After the war he worked as a commercial traveller in Vienna.

He also contacted the Red Cross International Tracing Service to try and find Citrónová, and he managed to track her to what had become Israel. In Israel, Citrónová married an Israel Defense Forces soldier, David Tahori, changed her name to Zippora Tahori and had two children.

Despite this, Wunsch wrote to her again and again, saying in one letter, "How completely different it would have been if we had won the war." She never responded to any of his letters – one of her relatives did write to him, telling him to stop, and invoking the names of Róza's children, telling him he had their blood on his hands. In the end, he too got married and started a family.

On 25 August 1971 Wunsch was arrested and tried at the second Vienna Auschwitz Trial, charged with war crimes. It was his wife who wrote to Helena Citrónová to ask her to testify – apparently he had never hidden his feelings for his great Auschwitz love. She had to decide whether to testify against Wunsch, at the potential cost of his life, when he had saved her sister's life. In the end she could only tell the truth – he had been kind to her, but she had witnessed first-hand his brutality to other prisoners.

At the end of the trial, Wunsch was allowed to walk free. He later claimed that he had been changed by his love for Citrónová. "I fell in love with Helena Citronova and that changed me. I changed into another person because of her influence." Citrónová died in Israel on 4 June 2007, and Wunsch died in Vienna on 23 February 2009.

There was no Hollywood ending – love and hope are both very messy things.

IT WAS VERY, VERY DANGEROUS

It is one of the most remarkable Auschwitz stories. Survivor Eva Clarke was conceived in a concentration camp, her mother's pregnancy was hidden from the Auschwitz authorities, and she was born at the gates of Mauthausen concentration camp – just a day after its gas chambers had been destroyed.

The story starts in 1933, when Bernd Nathan, a German-Jewish architect, left Hamburg for Prague after Hitler and the National Socialists came to power, part of the exodus of Jews from Germany. In Prague he met Anka Kauderová, a Czech Jew from Třebechovice, and they fell in love, marrying on 15 May 1940. A year and a half later, the couple were arrested and sent to Terezín (Theresienstadt).

Unusually, they were there for three years, their youth and fitness keeping them alive. The camp didn't have some of the more atrocious conditions that places like Auschwitz had and there were no gas chambers, but to survive so long in a Nazi concentration camp was remarkable for any individual, let alone a couple.

Even more remarkable was the fact that Anka fell pregnant with the baby she would name Eva. When Eva, as a teenager, asked her how she did so, given the segregation of the sexes, her mother replied, "Well, it was very, very dangerous, but…" Somehow, Bernd and Anka got together secretly any time they could, and "to hell with the consequences".

That child was not Eva but a boy who would be named Dan. When the authorities became aware that Anka was pregnant, she and Bernd were forced to sign a document stating that when the baby was born, it would have to be handed over to the Gestapo to be murdered. When Dan was born, Anka was allowed to nurse him, but then fate intervened, and he died of pneumonia aged two months.

Soon after, Bernd was sent on to Auschwitz. Astonishingly, Anka volunteered to go there too, and her wish was granted. What she did not know when she made the request was that she was pregnant again, with Eva. What followed was an astonishing threading of the needle by fate. On several occasions over the next few months a change of even a few days would have meant Eva – and probably her mother – would not have survived.

When she arrived at Auschwitz on 1 October 1944, nearly seven months before Eva's birth, Anka's pregnancy was not visible. When Josef Mengele asked her, as he did all new arrivals, if she was pregnant, she lied and said no – she was already aware of the child inside.

She was at Auschwitz for ten days, hoping nothing would give her away. She did not see Bernd in that time. Deemed fit for work, she was then, on 10 October, sent to work in a munitions factory in Freiberg, near Dresden. She was to be

IT WAS VERY, VERY DANGEROUS

there for six months, and during that time she became more and more visibly pregnant, especially as the meagre rations meant she weighed only 35 kilograms (5½ stone).

By the spring of 1945, the Germans were retreating and evacuating concentration and slave labour camps. Anka and her fellow munitions factory workers were placed in coal trains and driven around the country, lying on top of the coal, with no shelter above them. As with the death marches, the fraying Nazi army seemed to have no idea what to do with the camp survivors, and no administration or infrastructure to order their massacre or to carry it out.

Eventually, on 29 April, the train arrived at Mauthausen concentration camp. By then everyone arriving knew that the camp had gas chambers and she would have expected to be sent straight to them. The shock sent her into labour, and Eva was born on top of the coal truck without any medical assistance.

What Anka didn't know was that the gas chambers had been blown up the day before. Had they arrived 24 hours earlier they may have been among the last victims. What they also didn't know was that the Americans would liberate Mauthausen less than a week later on 5 May. By the time of its liberation, most of the guards in Mauthausen had fled; around 30 of those who remained were killed by the prisoners. An Army Signal Corps cameraman took film as evidence of Nazi atrocities. He also filmed Anka with her new baby, whom she had named Eva and had wrapped in paper as there was nothing else to put her in.

Even in her exhausted state, Anka helped during the liberation. She spoke fluent English, and she passed on warnings to the camp survivors from the US liberators that they should only eat very small amounts of food at a time – to eat a lot when you are severely malnourished as she herself was, could be fatal.

Three weeks later, Anka returned to Prague with her new daughter. She would later tell Eva that this was the worst moment of her three-and-a-half-year ordeal. For the first time she allowed herself to think about what had happened to her friends, family and all the other inmates. She wondered whether there would be anyone she knew left in Prague or in her hometown. There was one cousin, and Anka and her daughter found refuge with her for three years.

Anka soon found out what she had feared: Bernd had been murdered. It had happened on 10 January 1945, just days before Auschwitz was liberated by the Soviet army. He never knew his wife was pregnant.

She would later marry Karel Bergman, a Czech-Jewish military translator and member of the Royal Air Force during World War Two. Originally from Trhová Kamenice, he had emigrated to Britain in 1939 and returned to Czechoslovakia at the end of the war, having received multiple decorations for his service.

When Czechoslovakia fell into Communist – and therefore Soviet – control in 1948, the couple and Eva, whom Bergman had adopted, decided to leave and ended up in Cardiff, Wales, where Bergman had been offered a job. They were to spend the rest of their lives in Britain.

Eva Clarke has become one of Britain's most powerful Holocaust educators. After working as a college administrator in Cambridge for 20 years, she began speaking publicly of her family's experiences during the Holocaust and was awarded a British Empire Medal in 2019, "for services to Holocaust education".

In a strange twist of fate, when Eva married Malcolm Clarke, professor of law at Cambridge University, she was marrying a man whose father had been part of Bomber Command, which had attacked Dresden – where her mother, pregnant with Eva, was working in the munitions factory and sheltering from the bombs. As it was, Eva's mother lived to the age of 96.

Hope is sometimes a fragile thing – so many things could have been just slightly different and there would have been no Eva Clarke. A true case of the light of hope shining in the darkness.

THE FIVE-YEAR-OLD

"Human beings are built to have resilience. That's how we are made." – Tova Friedman

She was only five when she was taken to Auschwitz, one of thousands of children taken through those gates, and one of only a handful who would come back out. Tova Friedman's story of survival is a remarkable one – part luck, part resilience, and a testament to the power of hope.

She was born Tola Grossman on 7 September 1938, in Gdynia, Poland, close to Gdańsk, although her family was originally from the city of Tomaszów Mazowiecki, and a year after she was born, when war was declared, they moved back there.

In the city, the 5,000 Jewish residents were moved into a ghetto and immediately started dying in the cramped, unsanitary conditions. Others were shot, and many more were deported to the camps. Tova's family, living in a small apartment, was under constant threat of all three, and when children began being deported from the area, Tova's father made her hide in the crawlspace above their home's ceiling.

In 1944 they were arrested. At the train station, her father and mother were split up – he went to a train for men, she to a train for women, taking her daughter with her. Tova later found out that he was sent to Dachau, where he did hard labour. His wife and daughter were taken to Auschwitz.

It has been estimated that in the history of Auschwitz, around 232,000 children and young people (under the age of 16) were deported to the camp, of whom 216,000 were Jews, 11,000 Roma, about 3,000 Poles, more than 1,000 Belarusians and several hundred Russians, Ukrainians and others. When the camp was liberated only 700 remained.

On the train, there was only a small window up high, and Tova would remember that, being so small, the light never got down to her, so she kept falling asleep, with her head resting on the perspiring back of the woman in front of her.

She also remembered the smell – people were forced to go to the toilet where they stood, and as the smell grew worse they started throwing up, exacerbating the problem. Added to this was the sound of screaming – as a five-year-old, she would later say, she didn't know what death was, but the other women did, and they screamed for the whole train journey.

As the train doors were opened, she was struck by the bright light – and also the dogs, large German shepherds. Given her height, she found herself looking directly into the eyes of the dogs, and she could smell their saliva. She remembered telling her mother she thought the dogs would kill her, but her mother told her that they would only do so if she ran away.

THE FIVE-YEAR-OLD

Once in the camp, the five-year-old was asked to get undressed. She asked why. The guard told her that it was to check that she was healthy. She asked what would happen if she wasn't. The guard simply pointed to the chimneys with their billowing smoke.

She then went through the humiliation of being stripped, examined, placed in the striped uniform and having her head shaved. "You went as a person, as part of a family, and after they shaved you, you were not a human being. You were no longer yourself."

Unusually, Tova was not sent straight to the gas chamber, but to the Kinderlager or "children's camp". The ruthless efficiency of the Nazis in organizing extermination was beginning to crumble, but the children would soon end up in the crematorium – and they would have been aware of this. Locked in the barracks all day and night, the children could think of nothing but food, and death as far as they understood it.

She remembers a 12-year-old she shared a bed with who died. Twelve seemed impossibly old to her, and she was not surprised when the girl died – it became a game in the Kinderlager for children to predict how long others would live – two weeks, three weeks.

Tova had to remove the girl from the bed. She dragged her to where the other corpses were and told the guards her number, which she had remembered. "I was so proud of that," she later admitted.

She knew that her own death would be soon. She would later say that she thought that being Jewish meant you died – they went together. It was like, she said, how a five-year-old now knows they will go to kindergarten, just a normal part of life.

Then on 7 October, the inevitable came. The children knew something different was happening – they were given, according to Tova, "a delicious breakfast". Also those in the barrack next door had all been taken a few days before.

The children finished their breakfast, and then they were gathered together and marched to the gate of the gas chamber. This meant walking past the barracks of some of the women – including Tova's mother. Her mother called out to ask where she was going, and she told her she was going to the crematorium. Tova said she knew it was her mother without seeing her, because she used her name – which no one had done since she got to the camp.

The women, many of them who had children among the group, were all screaming and crying. Tova said she did not, because she knew every Jewish child goes to the crematorium.

The girls went into the chamber, and then a miracle, a glimmer of hope. For the one and only time in the history of Auschwitz, the gas chamber malfunctioned. It was later revealed that this was because the camp resistance had managed to set an explosive in the mechanism the day before. The damage was limited, but Tova Friedman at least owes her life to it.

Having left in the daylight, it was dark before the children were taken back – the guards had, it would seem, spent the day trying to get the chamber to work so the children could be killed. Again the children had to walk past the women, again the screaming and crying.

THE FIVE-YEAR-OLD

It was the first miracle escape, but it would not be the last. The next time was not due to sabotage, but due to a simple clerical error – for some reason Tova's number had been left off the list of those to die, so again having gone to the chamber, she was sent back to the barracks. The guards knew that some children were kept for Mengele to experiment on. Perhaps this five-year-old was being kept alive for that.

Then one day the guard in charge of the Kinderlager was gone. The children stayed inside, not sure what to do. But Tova heard her name being called – her mother forced her way in. Tova didn't recognize her at first – "She looked terrible" – and she had to convince the little girl that she was really her mother. She grabbed Tova and dragged her out of the barracks. It was snowing, and the death marches were about to begin. Anyone who didn't get in line fast enough was shot.

Tova's mother didn't want to get in the line. She had no shoes, she could barely stand. She told Tova that she was going to die on the road. Then she said words that Tova would always remember. "I don't want you to live alone in this world. I don't want you to survive by yourself. I want you to die with me here […] in Auschwitz."

Tova said yes – she believed that she and her mother were about to be shot.

But her mother managed to drag her to the infirmary. On the floor were piles of corpses. Tova's mother started touching each of the corpses. The five-year-old had no idea what she was doing. Then she came to a corpse that was still warm, which meant she could manipulate her body – the woman must have died minutes earlier.

She told Tova to climb into the pile and put her head under the armpit of the woman, with her mouth facing the ground so she could breathe. She manipulated the rest of Tova's body against the woman, and then covered them with a blanket, but with the hands sticking out the top to show she was dead. She told Tova to try not to breathe much or uncover herself. Tova started breathing as shallowly as possible.

She could hear the Nazis walking all around her, shooting anyone who was left. Someone stomped on the corpse Tova was under to check she was dead. Tova held her breath. The person moved on.

She remembered there was screaming, yelling and shooting, and then suddenly there was quiet. But there was also smoke. Fires were being set, but Tova, struggling to breathe, would not uncover herself. And just as she thought she could bear it no longer, the blanket was pulled back – it was her mother, who told her the Nazis were gone.

Tova looked around and saw more and more women emerging from under the corpses. The infirmary was burning, so they all walked outside – it was dark and still snowing. And the Germans were gone.

It was 25 January, and on 27 January the Russians arrived. They provided food and took photographs of the survivors, including an iconic one of a group of children. Tova is on the left of the picture, her sleeve rolled up, showing her tattoo. It appeared in newspapers and newsreels around the world, as people began to grapple with the realities of Auschwitz and the camps.

Tova and her mother returned to Poland, where they found that their home had been destroyed and most of the rest of

THE FIVE-YEAR-OLD

their extended family had been killed. Her father eventually returned from Dachau and they remained together in Poland for several years, before emigrating to the US. Tova studied psychology, receiving a Bachelor of Arts from Brooklyn University, and spent her working life as a therapist. She married and had four children, and many grandchildren, whose thoughts at five years old would have been all about starting kindergarten. Hope had triumphed against all the odds.

DESIGNING WOMAN

As we read about all the horrors of the Holocaust, it is possible for even the most sensitive person to become desensitized to the little ways in which the Nazis went about dehumanizing the Jews. We all know about the yellow star, but few of us let that sink in.

Mady Gerrard was 13 in 1944 when her hometown in Hungary came under Nazi control and Nazi laws. She was banned from going to school as her parents were banned from working. Having to wear, and to see her parents wear, the yellow star was, she told the BBC in 2020, the "cruellest and most humiliating" of the Nazi policies.

But then Mady always had an eye for the symbolism in what we wear. In her life after the war, as a British citizen after a brief time back in Hungary, she would develop a fashion brand of crocheted and painted silk garments which made her world famous – presidents and celebrities wore her designs.

Although she spent most of her time during the war in Bergen-Belsen, when she was in Auschwitz she was put to work making aeroplane parts. Here she saw a chance to express herself and bring hope to the other inmates. Using a twig as a knitting needle and pieces of wire that she found, she fashioned necklaces. These she gave to the other women around her, to wear in secret when they could.

Given her creativity, Mady was asked in Auschwitz to make socks for a woman named Molly, who was from her hometown. Molly's feet were freezing in the cold of the camp, but Mady said she couldn't help as she had no wool. Then someone had the idea that fir needles woven together might work, and her friends gathered as many as they could. Molly got her socks.

It was in April 1945 that relief came. The British arrived at Belsen, where Mady had been moved to in a horrific death march, and released them. "We knew it was liberation," she said, "and we thought it was wonderful, because we knew we only had a few days left to live." The conditions had been so brutal she would later say that she would wish them on no one, Hitler included.

By then, of course, Adolf Hitler was dead. But Mady Gerrard was not.

She moved to Cardiff in 1956 and became a British citizen soon after. Before her death in 2021 she had three grandchildren, and two great-grandchildren and a huge reputation in the fashion industry. For her, fashion was always about human connection, just like those necklaces and socks she made in Auschwitz. Proof that the human spirit will always fight those who try to kill it.

THE COST OF AN ORANGE

On 8 May 1989, Gerda Weissmann Klein celebrated her 65th birthday. That date is, of course a historic one for all those who suffered under Hitler – it is VE Day, the day that Germany surrendered in 1945. But for Gerda it had even greater resonance. Her story starts before her parents were taken to Auschwitz, but it is still part of the story of the camp.

On her 65th birthday, at her home in Arizona, Gerda was surrounded by friends and family. But there was also one very special guest, a woman who had been at Gerda's 18th birthday party as well – in the ghetto in Bielsko, Poland, where Gerda and her family were living in forced detention under the Nazis. Any attempt to leave the ghetto could lead to execution.

Klein remembered that the party was "rather grand" – her mother had managed to make oatmeal from the meagre rations they received, which the girls at the party ate gratefully.

But it was her present that Gerda still remembered with wide-eyed excitement, talking about it after nearly 50 years. Her parents gave her "an incredible thing" – an orange. This was an unheard-of luxury in the ghetto.

It was only later that she found out that to get the orange, her mother had made a dangerous, potentially deadly trip outside the ghetto in the middle of the night, and sold a diamond and pearl ring to get the orange. And, it was the last birthday gift from her parents.

Soon afterwards Gerda's father, Julius Weissmann, was taken away to Auschwitz. He had suffered a heart attack the year before, which had stopped them escaping from Poland. Unfit for work, he was immediately sent to the gas chamber. And then they came for Gerda and her mother.

Gerda was deemed fit for work and so was destined for a labour camp; her mother Helene was not, and so she was sent to Auschwitz. As they were being separated, Gerda tried to stay with her mother. The head of the local Jewish Council, the Judenrat, pulled her away and placed her in the labour van, saying, "You are too young to die."

She spent much of the rest of the war carrying out back-breaking work in a textile mill in Bolkenhain, Silesia. The women there, joined in deprivation, and many of them in the knowledge that their parents were dead, formed a sort of community, which sometimes included those in charge – the textile mill managed in many ways to avoid the usual scrutiny. Gerda recalled one occasion when she was sick and had gone to the camp hospital. The factory supervisor, Mrs Kugler, heard that an SS man was due to make an inspection and that the sick would be gassed. She dragged Gerda out of the hospital, put her in front of a loom and set her going just as the SS arrived. Gerda was delirious from fever, but she passed the inspection.

THE COST OF AN ORANGE

Gerda was later sent to slave-labour camps in Merzdorf and Landshut. As was becoming normal in the last days of the Third Reich, she was also sent on a pointless death march. No one knew what to do with the remaining inmates. This march nearly ended in a massacre. The SS locked about a hundred women, including Gerda, in a factory in Volary, in what is now the Czech Republic, and set explosives and a timer with the intention of killing them all. But they left the timer outside – rain came, and it failed to go off.

It was from Volary that Gerda was liberated in May 1945 by US forces, one of whom was Lieutenant Kurt Klein. They had something in common – he had fled Germany in 1937, and his parents had also been murdered in Auschwitz. They fell in love, and in 1946 married in Paris.

They moved to Buffalo, US, and raised three children. Gerda became a journalist and wrote a series of books about her experiences. In 1995, a film was made based on her autobiography, *All But My Life*, which won an Academy Award for best short documentary. She also founded an organization called Citizenship Counts in 2008, which taught young people the rights and responsibilities of citizenship, and in 2011 was awarded the Presidential Medal of Freedom, the highest honour in the US. In his speech presenting the medal, Barack Obama said of Gerda, "She has taught the world that it is often in our most hopeless moments that we discover the extent of our strength and the depth of our love."

But it was something that she said on accepting her Academy Award that perhaps shows where we can look to find hope and joy, even in things we take for granted: "In my mind's eye I see those years and days and those who never lived to see the magic of a boring evening at home."

Hope and joy can still be found in boring evenings at home. And in something as simple as an orange.

BANNED WORDS

Polish-born Auschwitz survivor Leon Weintraub has two words that he banned from his vocabulary and will not stand to hear said in his presence. One is the word "hate" and the other is the word "revenge". These are words, he says, that have caused so much damage.

He was born in Łódź, Poland on 1 January 1926, as the fifth child to a Jewish family. Before he was two his father died, and he and his siblings – four sisters – were raised by his mother. Without a father to provide for them, the family lived in poverty, in only two rooms. The tables would become beds at night, he told the Berlin Guides Association in 2024. One of Leon's first responsibilities was to set their dog on the landlord when he came to collect the rent.

At the age of 13, Leon had only ever seen German soldiers in films, and they were always portrayed as noble and heroic. But when the German Army swept through Poland on 1 September 1940, and into Łódź, he soon found they were far from that.

All Jewish families were rounded up and taken to ghettos, where they lived as prisoners. The Łódź ghetto was overseen by the Head of the Jewish Council of Elders in the city, Chaim Mordechai Rumkowski, who attempted to balance Nazi demands with the needs of his people and seemed increasingly to prioritize the former over the latter, to the point he was accused of being a collaborationist or even a traitor. He believed that if he acceded to German demands and supplied labour to the camps, they would feel compelled to keep the Jews alive. Rumkowski was wrong, and he himself would be sent to Auschwitz in 1944, where he was killed by other Jewish inmates on 28 August.

Leon described the poverty of the ghetto, which was even worse than what he had suffered at home. The population got one piece of bread, about 2 kilograms (4 ½ pounds) per head per person, per week. "In summertime it was mostly bad potatoes, and in the wintertime, frozen potatoes."

On 4 September 1942, Rumkowski announced that he had been ordered to deport the weak, elderly and the young. He gave a speech that would become notorious, ending with the words, "Fathers and mothers, give me your children."

Leon and his family were spared – for now – and Leon worked in a steel-making factory, producing parts for the German army. But as food supplies started to run out, more and more people were rounded up and taken from the ghettos to the concentration camps. In addition, the Soviet army was closing in on Łódź. The Germans decided to retreat, but wanted to shut the ghetto down first, so everyone was to be deported.

Leon and his family tried to hide, but in August they were captured and taken to a cattle car – they were being sent to Auschwitz.

BANNED WORDS

As soon as they arrived, the selection took place. Leon's mother and one of his sisters were immediately sent to the left – the gas chambers. Leon, stripped, shaved and dressed in his prison outfit, was sent to Block 10. With the high volume of executions, not everyone could be gassed straight away, and Block 10 functioned as a holding cell for those who had been deemed unfit for work but who could wait for gassing. He was not registered and so was not given a tattoo.

He was stuck in Block 10, but he managed occasionally to go outside. One day he saw between Block 16 and 18 a big group of naked men. He asked them, "What are you doing here naked?" He was told they were waiting for clothes before being sent out to work. Leon immediately put away his shirt, jacket and trousers, and mixed deep in this group of naked people.

It was a spilt-second decision that would save his life. Soon after, a family friend, who also survived Auschwitz, saw everyone from Block 10 taken to the gas chamber – he assumed the group had included Leon.

Instead, Leon was on a train with the previously naked men, being sent northwest to the Gross-Rosen camp in the neighbouring state of Lower Silesia. Although the camp had no gas chambers, conditions remained harsh, and much of his early work was helping to dig giant tunnels which firms like IG Farben could put factories in to protect them from Allied bombing. The men worked without proper tools, and these tunnels were always in danger of collapse.

Another bit of quick thinking saved Leon on another occasion. The guards asked if there were any electricians among the workers. Leon immediately told them that he was an electrician – a bald-faced lie. But it meant that he could stop the back-breaking work and pretend to be working on the electrics for the tunnel system. He was able to loiter underground for periods too and alter his badge without anyone seeing in order to get better rations, which he could share with the other men. He knew that if he was caught doing any of these things he would be hanged – he knew because he had seen it.

But the Soviet army, which had chased him out of Łódź, now started approaching the Gross-Rosen camp. The camp was evacuated. The prisoners were sent on a death march, and then placed on a train to yet another concentration camp, Flossenbürg, Leon's third in a year. Formerly a quarry, it was now being used for arms production. As with all of the concentration camps in the final days of the war, it was hideously overcrowded, as the Germans tried to absorb new arrivals from camps that were being destroyed.

It was also cold. In the middle of winter, without winter clothes – without anything much in the way of clothes at all – large numbers of the inmates fell ill, Leon included, and many more died. On 22 March he was moved again in the futile rounds of transportation of the last days of Nazism, finding himself at his fourth concentration camp, Natzweiler-Struthof. He was only there briefly, before once again being ordered onto a train.

It was to be his final journey as a Nazi prisoner. The train was passing through the Black Forest when it came under enemy bombardment, and the engine was damaged. Everyone was told to get out. They all stood around for a while, and then the SS guards suddenly decided en masse to run away. The bemused inmates watched them go and then ran in the opposite direction.

When they got to safety, Leon was taken to a French hospital. He was in such a bad state that he was to stay there for two months – his weight was down to 35 kilograms (5½ stone) and he was suffering from typhus. Once he had recuperated, he returned home, surprising all of those who believed he had been killed in the extermination of Block 10, and himself being surprised to find three of his sisters, who had survived Bergen-Belsen.

Shortly after the war Leon met his wife, Katia Hof, and went on to have three sons. To bring them into the world was a triumph of hope, but Leon wanted more. He decided to study to be a gynaecologist so he could bring more babies into the world, many of them Jewish – just what the Nazis and men like Josef Mengele had tried to stop. He became chief of staff of a hospital just outside Warsaw.

In 1969, with a new rise in anti-Semitism in Eastern Europe, Leon and his family left Poland and moved to Sweden. Katia died in 1970 and six years later he was remarried, to Evamaria.

And on the 80th anniversary of the liberation of Auschwitz, Leon Weintraub was one of the key speakers. As ever, there were two words he did not use – hate and revenge.

THE DANCER

What is hope? How does it manifest itself? As we have seen, it takes many forms – and one of the most powerful is the human spirit that can survive even the horrors of Auschwitz. And as we know, part of what makes up the human spirt is our creativity – in music, in poetry. And as Helen Lewis proves, in dance.

This dancer was born Helena Katz in 1916 into a German-speaking Jewish family in Trutnov in Bohemia, Austria-Hungary (now in the Czech Republic). In 1934 her father died, and she and her mother moved to Prague, where she studied dance with the renowned teacher Milča Mayerová, as well as studying philosophy and French. In 1936 she met her future husband, Paul Hermann, a Jew from what was then Czechoslovakia. In 1938, after she had finished her dance training and her university exams, they were married and Helena began teaching dance to private students.

In 1939, Czechoslovakia was overrun by the Nazis, and in 1941 the deportations of the Jews began. Helena and Paul were sent in 1942 to Terezín and separated. Helena began work in a children's home within the camp, where she tried to teach dance while living in a barrack room with 30 other women, five to a bunk. While there she suffered from acute appendicitis but somehow survived.

Two years later, in May 1944, they were transferred to Auschwitz and separated once more. They would never see each other again. In 1945 Paul was transferred to Schwarzheide concentration camp and died in the March. Helena survived being selected twice by Josef Mengele and used in medical experiments.

Helena was moved again, this time to Stutthof concentration camp and was put to back-breaking work in the snow. When the camp was closed in January 1945, she was sent on a death march with several hundred other women – without an agreed destination. Eventually, after two weeks, they were simply placed in an abandoned barn. Three days passed, and then they were ordered to march again. By now the guards were as tired as the prisoners, and Helena was able to jump in a ditch and escape.

She reached a nearby house and remained there until the Russian army liberated the village. She was eventually able to get to hospital, where she slowly recovered, and when the war ended, she returned to Prague, where she learned of her husband's death; her mother, who had been deported early in 1942, had been murdered at Sobibór extermination camp.

But that is not the end of the story of Helena Katz. She was about to remind the world of the strength of the human spirit.

In 1947, Helena married a friend, Harry Lewis, who had escaped to Northern Ireland from Prague before the war, and moved with him to Belfast. Although no longer able to

THE DANCER

dance due to the ravages of her health, Helena – now Helen – worked as a choreographer and dance teacher. She rebuilt her career by beginning with small venues, and by 1956 she had become one of the leading choreographers in Northern Ireland. Her choreography of *The Golden Spinning Wheel* by the Czech composer Dvořák at the Belfast Ballet Club that year is considered the first modern dance performance in the history of Northern Ireland. She collaborated closely with the internationally acclaimed director Sam McCready, a founder member of the world famous Lyric Theatre in Belfast, where many of their productions took place. She became the resident choreographer there, producing some of the greatest works in Northern Irish history, from the opening production of four plays from W. B. Yeats's *Cuchulain Cycle* in 1968, through to *A Time to Remember* in 2000.

Helen also founded the Belfast Modern Dance Group in 1962, which became the "focus for performing arts" in Northern Ireland during the Troubles, and in 2001 she was awarded an MBE. A dance studio at the Crescent Arts Centre in Belfast is named after her. Her memoir, *A Time to Speak*, about her experiences before and during the war, was published in 1992. Translated into many languages, it was also adapted for the stage by McCready.

Helen Lewis died in 2009 at the age of 93. She had outlived the Nazi regime by 64 years, and she spent those 64 years creating artwork that not only made her famous but explored and celebrated the human spirit. The woman the Nazis had tried to kill had danced her way into thousands of hearts.

NIGHT

Perhaps no one has been so associated with Auschwitz, survival and hope as Elie Wiesel. His memoir, *Night*, documenting his time in Auschwitz and Buchenwald, is seen as one of the great classics not only of Holocaust literature but of all twentieth-century literature. In a mere 116 pages, it takes the reader on a journey of emotions, from anger to despair to sadness and to hope. So profound was its impact that Wiesel became a universal symbol of all those who had died in the Holocaust, and those who had survived.

In fact, *Night* is the first book in a trilogy of memoirs, *Night*, *Dawn* and *Day*, which Wiesel said was his way of representing a move from darkness to light, drawing on the Jewish tradition of a new day starting in the evening.

Published in 1956, only a decade after the end of the war, when the world was still categorizing what had happened into black and white, *Night* was shocking in its complex and nuanced examination of an event almost beyond human understanding.

Wiesel himself was born to a Jewish family in Sighet in the Carpathian Mountains of Romania. His was an educated family – they spoke Yiddish most of the time, but also

German, Hungarian and Romanian. His mother Sarah was devout and encouraged him to read the Torah, while his father Shlomo encouraged him to learn Hebrew and to read great literature. His life and art would become a mixture of these two influences.

He had three sisters – two older, Beatrice and Hilda, and one younger, Tzipora. For the most part they had been able to avoid the war, although anti-Semitism in what was then Hungary was rife. Then, like for so many Hungarian Jews, the victory of what was essentially a Nazi puppet regime, the Arrow Cross Party, saw the yoke of racial laws descend – and saw the deportations to the death camps begin.

The Wiesel family were rounded up, and after a brief stay in the Sighet ghetto, they were sent to Auschwitz. Wiesel – called "Eliezer" in the book – and his father then went through the dehumanizing processes of Auschwitz: the head shaving, the examination, the tattooing, all recorded in the memoir. It was the first time that the young boy had seen his father as anything but a strong man, and much of the rest of *Night* is an exploration of their relationship – Shlomo becoming smaller and weaker, and his son, still growing at 16, becoming his carer and having to look after him, which shames them both. Wiesel also resents his father, whose existence makes his own survival more difficult, as he is now tied to the fate of a man wasting away. He briefly thinks about throwing himself against the electric fence, and is about to do so when everyone is called back to the barracks. He has not died but as the memoir makes clear, something inside him has died – the child he was, and the faith he had in God.

NIGHT

Wiesel is unflinching about his own failings and those of his father. He is also unflinching when he confronts his guilt – in some sense, he wishes his father dead, so he himself will be free, and so he can go back to the father he knew before Auschwitz, strong and in charge. Not the weak man crying in the bunk.

As with other men, Wiesel and his father were selected to perform labour so long as they remained able-bodied, after which they were to be murdered in the gas chambers. Wiesel found himself having to help his father despite his own suffering, with the knowledge that if his father failed, he would die. He struggled to complete his own tasks, but as he was to say after the war, his primary motivation for carrying on was to keep his father alive.

In August 1944, the pair were transferred to the work camp at Monowitz.

There was a brief moment of joy when the camp was bombed by the Americans, and for the first time they saw their Nazi oppressors running around in terror – the fear that up until then they had only seen in their comrades.

It was also here that Wiesel, according to *Night*, began to explore his relationship with faith. On one occasion the camp was called together to watch a child being hanged as punishment – no one was allowed to look away, under threat of being next. Not heavy enough for the weight of his body to break his neck, the boy died slowly. As he did, Wiesel heard someone behind him ask where God was now, to which he replied he was there, hanging on the gallows.

STORIES OF HOPE FROM AUSCHWITZ

He was in a battle with his faith. He was unable to take part in the Rosh Hashanah, the Jewish New Year, as he couldn't bring himself to bless God – only curse him.

In January 1945, Wiesel and his father were forced to join one of the death marches, as the Nazis shut down the camp and tried to remove evidence of their crimes, including the starving Jews. The two men were among those marched to Gleiwitz to be put on a freight train to Buchenwald, a camp near Weimar, Germany, 563 kilometres (350 miles) from Auschwitz. On the walk, anyone who staggered, stumbled or sat down was immediately shot.

The train to Buchenwald took ten days and nights – with no water, no food. Only melting snow leaking in through the cracks in the walls provided any sustenance. According to the memoir, only 12 of the 100 or so men who boarded the train survived the journey.

As they got off the train, his father stumbled and Wiesel found himself yelling at him to move. He eventually left his father, as the barracks were about to close, and to be outside risked being shot. In the morning, as he went to look for Shlomo, he recognized that a part of him hoped that his father was dead.

Remarkably, Shlomo was alive, and was moved to the bunk below his son. Wiesel heard him being beaten by other inmates for not going out to the toilet and soiling the barracks. Wiesel could only listen. And then one night his father begged for water and an SS man hit him on the head with a truncheon for making a noise. The next morning when Wiesel woke, he was gone, replaced by another man.

Three months later Buchenwald was liberated.

NIGHT

At the end of the war, Elie Wiesel, still only 17, was sent to France, where he learned that his two older sisters Beatrice and Hilda had also survived the war – unlike Tzipora who had been gassed aged seven – and was reunited with them at a French orphanage. Hilda later emigrated to the US, and Beatrice to Canada. Wiesel studied literature, philosophy and psychology at the Sorbonne under teachers such as the famous French philosopher Jean-Paul Sartre. At 19 he became a journalist. He was hired as Paris correspondent for the Israeli newspaper *Yedioth Ahronoth*, subsequently becoming its roaming international correspondent.

For ten years he wrote nothing about his time in the camps. But then on the encouragement of the author François Mauriac, winner of the 1952 Nobel Prize for Literature, he decided to try and capture what he had been through. The result was a 900-page memoir, written in Yiddish, called *And the World Remained Silent*. Wiesel took out all his anger in his writing, but it did not make for a good book. He started to cut it down and down, and the more he cut the more his vision of what he wanted to say came into focus. Wiesel rewrote a shortened version of the manuscript in French, *La Nuit*, in 1955. In 1960, it was rewritten as *Night*, in English, the first of 30 languages it would be translated into.

The book was not an immediate success, but its popularity eventually blossomed, and it has now sold some 10 million copies in the US alone. The book appears on school curriculums throughout the world.

Wiesel himself moved to the US in 1969, marrying Marion Rose, with whom he had a son, whom he named Shlomo after his father.

STORIES OF HOPE FROM AUSCHWITZ

Wiesel was awarded the Nobel Peace Prize in 1986 for speaking out against violence, repression and racism. The Nobel Committee, in its commendation, described Wiesel as one of the most important spiritual leaders and guides in an age when violence, repression and racism continue to characterize the world, and called him a messenger to mankind. His speech in accepting the award was one of hope but also of defiance, and a call to courage in the face of violence and oppression.

Wiesel is also a well-known advocate of the rights of refugees, coining the phrase "No human being is illegal" when confronted with the idea of "illegal aliens".

For the rest of his life he continued to fight for the rights of the oppressed against the oppressor. It was a battle that had begun in Auschwitz, when he saw first-hand how even the strongest can be broken down by brutality and how the weakest use brutality to try and make themselves appear strong. But he was in no doubt that those who do the worst things can be defeated, like the Nazis. As he put it, "The opposite of love is not hate, it's indifference."

THE BAR MITZVAH

It is one of the most important moments in the life of any Jewish boy – the bar mitzvah. Celebrated for hundreds of years, it symbolizes a young boy's coming of age, and thus the fact that he takes responsibility for his actions. Before he turns 13 they are the responsibility of his parents; after the bar mitzvah they are his alone. The equivalent ceremony for girls is the bat mitzvah.

But what do you do when your bar mitzvah falls on a day when you are on a cattle truck being moved from Auschwitz to the Kraków-Płaszów concentration camp?

David Bergman, known as Dudi, was born on 3 May 1931, in a small town in Ruthenia, Czechoslovakia's easternmost province. His father was a tailor and his mother was a seamstress.

The town was so remote that any news from the outside was announced by a drummer in the main square, who would summon the townsfolk and then let them know what was going on. And from 1933 what was delivered was mostly the drumbeats of war.

The first time the Bergmans were directly affected was in March 1939. They had a Czech soldier living with them, but the annexation of Czechoslovakia by Hungary had begun, and the soldier fled. David suddenly found himself having to pledge allegiance to Hungary at school.

The next five years were spent in the shadow of war, as the noose continued to tighten around the Jews of Europe, Czechoslovakia included. And in 1944, David and his father could no longer escape. They were taken first to Auschwitz, where they stayed for five days, and then they were reassigned, to be sent on to Kraków-Płaszów. They were among about 15 men being transported.

Once the train started, David's father made an announcement – today was the day of his son's bar mitzvah, the day of taking responsibility, of becoming a man. Somehow, he had hidden on himself a small bottle of wine. David never found out how, or where it had come from. Surely he had not acquired it at Auschwitz, but surely he had not kept it with him since their arrest, just for this occasion?

His father took the bottle of wine and passed it around. Everybody took a sip and said a toast. This was his bar mitzvah.

Speaking about it years later, for all that it was a celebration, David Bergman said, "It was very sad." But, he added, "There was no time to think then of this, the time then was [about] survival."

And survive David did, although often only just – unlike his father, who was killed shortly after his son's bar mitzvah. Moved from Kraków-Płaszów, David was sent to the Reichenbach camp. As is so often the case with stories of the last year of the war, apart from the barbarity, there was a futility to all of these transports and death marches.

THE BAR MITZVAH

But it was on his final journey in 1945 that 13-year-old David came probably as close to death as it is possible to come. He and 150 other Reichenbach inmates were put on a train to be sent to the concentration camp in Dachau, all 150 in a single cattle car. They travelled for four days without food or water. Already starving before they left, almost immediately men started dying, collapsing to the floor where they stood. It was, David later recounted, possible to sit down on a seat of corpses.

At one point a dying man fell against him. David had to use all of his remaining strength to push him off and then fell on top of him. The man tried to fight him off in any way he could and sunk his teeth into David's leg. It was the man's final moment – he died and fell away.

The hell wasn't over when David arrived at Dachau. It turned out that of the 150 men who had been placed on the train, only three survived, including David. The camp authorities believed all the men were dead and forced the inmates to start to move the bodies to the crematorium for burning.

David described himself being thrown onto a stretcher when someone noticed his arm move. Realizing he was alive, the inmates waited for the guards to be busy elsewhere and snuck the boy into the camp facilities, such as they were. David woke in completely unfamiliar surroundings, completely dazed and, like his captors, believing he was dead.

To those at the camp he became a sort of hero, a symbol of life. They told him that if he had survived, then maybe their sons, sent in the other direction from Dachau, might have done so too. They kept him hidden, and the camp authorities had no idea he was there. This meant he did not receive rations, so each man shared a piece of his single slice of bread each day to keep this symbol of hope alive.

It was in May 1945 that he was finally liberated. One day the SS simply evacuated the camp, leaving the inmates to wander out. David and ten others walked up a hill to see a way out. Suddenly military vehicles arrived, pouring into the camp. One of the men on the hill said he would give someone all of his food if they would go down and see who it was, knowing if they were Americans he would be free, but if not he would be back in captivity.

They were Americans. He was free.

David emigrated to the US in 1947. He had survived, and responsibility for his life no longer belonged to the Nazis.

THE BABY AT THE TRAIN STATION

We can never know what they felt at that moment, because no one survived to tell us.

They were not told what was about to happen, although there were doubtless rumours, and the stench of death was everywhere. On arrival at the camp, they were informed they would first have to undergo disinfection and bathe in special bunkers near the station. Those who were able to walk went on foot, those too incapacitated were carried on trucks.

Then they undressed. If they were going to crematorium I, they undressed in a yard with a wall around it. Those going to crematoria II, III, IV and V went to a special undressing room. If the numbers going to crematorium V were too large, as was increasingly the case from 1944 onwards, some undressed in the open air.

Then the doors of the gas chamber opened. It was at this point that many must have realized what was going to happen. As one Auschwitz survivor, Romanian doctor Charles Bendel, described it in October 1945, panic would often set in. The guards began to herd the men, women and children in with whips and sticks.

Within 2 minutes, the gas Zyklon B had been pumped into the chamber. Penetrating the lungs through inhalation, Zyklon B caused excruciating pain, violent convulsions and, finally, a heart attack.

Bendel said that after a time the doors would be opened. Bodies, tightly jammed inside, would begin to fall out. The corpses were then looted for jewellery and teeth. Then they were burned – cremation is forbidden in Jewish law, a final insult – and the remains dumped into mass graves in time for another convoy to arrive and start to undress.

Did Marta Knapp know what was about to happen? She and her husband Alexandr had been fleeing Prague, Czechoslovakia, in June 1942 with their baby daughter Alice when Nazi soldiers boarded the train at a place called Pardubice. Being Jewish, the couple knew they were about to be arrested, which they knew meant being sent to the camps. They made a split-second decision. One of them, we will never know which, jumped from the train, placed Alice on a bench on the train station, and got back on the train.

From there they were taken to Theresienstadt, and then on to Auschwitz, where they went to the gas chambers. As Marta walked through those doors, she must have thought about her little girl and the fact that she wasn't making the same journey. But was she safe?

She was. The baby girl had been picked up and taken to an orphanage. In 2022, Alice Grusová (her married name) celebrated her 81st birthday – as well as her 60th wedding anniversary with husband Miroslav – in Prague, the city her

THE BABY AT THE TRAIN STATION

parents had fled all those years ago. She and Miroslav had three sons, six grandchildren and three great-grandchildren. So many people owe their lives to that split-second decision.

But there is even more to this remarkable story, some of it tragic, some of it beautiful, like life itself. Shortly after the war Alice was somehow – she doesn't know how – reunited with her mother's younger sister Edith, who had survived Auschwitz.

They only lived together for two years, with Alice in Edith's care, but then one day Edith left for what was then Palestine, and six-year-old Alice was put up for adoption. Alice was devastated and didn't understand why her aunt didn't take her with her.

They stayed in touch for a while. Alice knew her aunt had got married and had a son, but in the middle of the 1960s the correspondence ended. Alice married and moved on.

Then in 2021 she received an email. A woman named Michalya Schonwald Moss was tracing her family and had stumbled upon her story. Did Alice know she had a cousin? His name was Yossi Weiss, he was 67, and he was living in the Israeli city of Haifa.

Edith's son.

They wanted to meet, but Yossi had cancer so couldn't travel. So, at 80, Alice went to Israel. There she met her cousin and learned more about his mother, her aunt Edith. Neither Alice nor Yossi could understand why Edith had given Alice up for adoption, but they tried – she had been so young when trying to care for a child who was not her own. In the end they forgave her.

STORIES OF HOPE FROM AUSCHWITZ

Yossi was also able to reveal why correspondence had stopped – Edith had committed suicide. Life had obviously become too much to bear. She was another victim of Auschwitz.

But Alice's family, Edith's family, and that of Alice's parents, Marta and Alexandr Knapp, goes on. Hope lives.

HANNA'S DOLL

It became an iconic image – taken on 5 July 1939 and listed in the photographer's notes simply as "Three little children waiting at Liverpool Street Station". The three girls were on one of the first Kindertransports from Germany to England and were shown sitting on a wooden seat – two on the left of the photo with knee socks and what all the papers described as Shirley Temple curls, one of them giving a big smile, and on the right, an older girl with pigtails, in a black mackintosh, holding a doll. To the press it was a perfect example of Britain's charity compared to the evils of Nazi Germany.

But it was not until 2001, when the historian Martin Gilbert published his book *Never Again: A History of the Holocaust*, that the picture took on a life of its own. It was reproduced in the book, began appearing in more and more places online, and then as part of a great many photographic exhibitions as the various anniversaries of World War Two occurred.

But – who were the girls?

When Inge Adamecz Hamilton bought Gilbert's book soon after it came out, she was in for a shock. Looking at the pictures, she came across the one of the three little girls. She knew immediately who two of them were – the little smiling girl was her, and the girl on the left was her sister Ruth. "That was a big surprise," Inge told the BBC. She contacted the author. "I wrote to him and said we are very much alive."

Inge had no memory of her journey on the Kindertransport and remembered very little of what had come before. The five-year-old had fled her home in Breslau, Germany, now Wrocław in Poland, with her seven-year-old sister Ruth. Their mother and younger sister had stayed behind and were murdered at Auschwitz.

That younger sister, Gretel, appears in a family photo of the three girls. Too young to travel, she must have been no more than five when she went to the gas chamber.

But who was the third girl holding the doll?

Twin sisters Debbie and Helen Singer had been coming at the problem from the other end. Their mother Hanna had first seen the picture in an exhibition at Camden Library in London to mark the 50th anniversary of the Kindertransport in 1989. She sent a copy to her daughters.

In 2023 BBC Radio 4 broadcast a documentary, *The Girls: The Holocaust Safe House*, telling the story of a hostel in Tyneside, in the north of England, where Inge and Ruth had ended up. The same photograph was used to promote the documentary. As a result, more information was found.

Hanna had in fact come to England with her twin brother Gerald, whose leg can be seen on the right of the photograph. Her mother was also able to come to England,

HANNA'S DOLL

on a sponsored domestic visa. Her father was not so lucky – he was murdered in Auschwitz.

Hanna met and married another refugee from Nazi Germany – Peter Singer, who had arrived in 1937 to go to school. They married in 1955, and Debbie and Helen were born in 1958.

Hanna became an English teacher.

And the doll? Children on the Kindertransport were allowed to carry very little with them – all of the girls in the photo have a small bag, which held all of their worldly possessions. But Hanna's doll, named Evelyn, just had to come. The photograph shows the moment when Hanna showed Inge the doll – the smile was one of pure happiness.

Hanna died in 2018, and Ruth had already passed in 2015. But Inge and the twin daughters of Hanna got in touch with each other and met up at the Imperial War Museum in 2023, 84 years after the photo was taken.

Debbie and Helen now advocate for refugee rights in memory of when England came together to save three girls – and about 9,997 other children – from the horrors of Auschwitz and the camps.

THE ELDER

It was an almost impossible line to walk. In *The Drowned and the Saved*, Primo Levi called it the "grey zone" – so much of what happened in Auschwitz was in a zone of moral ambiguity. People forced to survive cannot make the choices they would like to make, or would make in normal life. No one who has not experienced such deprivation has any right to judge.

One of the tricks of the camps – for both organizational and propaganda purposes – was to install camp elders. As the name suggests, these were usually older men or women inmates (older, but still young enough to work) chosen to run the day-to-day affairs of each unit – leadership positions within a subjugated population.

The individuals in these positions held a certain degree of power – a great degree compared to those around them – but remained subject to the SS guards and the rules of the camp. They also had some influence – and the trick was to use this as best they could.

Magda Hellinger was 26 when she arrived at Auschwitz in 1942. She had been a kindergarten teacher in Czechoslovakia before her arrest. Her father had been a schoolteacher, teaching Jewish history and German, which meant that Hellinger was fluent in German. This would be useful in the camps – first in terms of keeping her alive, and second in the role she was given. She had also been active in Zionist movements and had worked as an assistant to a physician, which gave her basic first aid skills – which she would also put to use.

When she was eight, she had had a strange encounter with a rabbi. He told her mother that she would "save hundreds and hundreds of Jewish souls". This would become her mantra when she reached the camp.

She arrived at a historic time in the history of Auschwitz. Until 1942, the camp had not been exclusively Jewish – in fact, it had mostly been used for Polish political prisoners and enemy prisoners of war, including Poles and Soviets. The first mass transport had arrived in 1940, containing 728 male Polish political prisoners. The first gassing took place in August 1941, of a group of Soviet prisoners, followed by another 600, plus 250 Poles, that September.

It was soon after this, in January 1942, that the notorious Wannsee Conference was held in a suburb of Berlin. During the meeting, for the first time (at least officially), plans for the "Final Solution to the Jewish Question" were laid out and agreed upon. The Jews were to be exterminated – this was what would later come to be called genocide. And Auschwitz, the gas chambers having proved effective, was to be one of the main centres for doing so.

On 20 March 1942, Magda Hellinger was in one of the first intakes of Jews into the camp. As with all new arrivals,

THE ELDER

she went through the selection process, being chosen to queue to the right with others capable of work, and not to the left, with those going to the gas chamber. She then went to the tattooist and received her number, by which she would be known – inmates were only ever called by their number, not their name.

Except she wasn't. She was selected soon after to be a camp elder – "not a job you could turn down" she later wrote – and as the title of her memoir makes clear, things were different for her. The book is *The Nazis Knew My Name*. They called her Magda. And in that simple gesture she took some of their power.

Later in 1942 she was moved to the women's camp at Birkenau, and her good German and gutsiness won the respect of SS guards and their bosses. One of them, Irma Grese, began to rely on her as a confidante. Grese was notorious for the way she treated prisoners and became known as the Hyena of Auschwitz. Wielding a rubber truncheon, pistol and whip, she took delight in beating and torturing the women under her command. Some estimates say she killed up to 30 women a day at the height of her power.

She was also known to indulge in sadistic sex with inmates. Having already had an affair with Josef Mengele, whose experiments on children made him one of the most reviled Nazis, she was said to take sadistic pleasure in watching women be experimented on.

At the end of the war Grese was tried and sentenced to death, her arrogant manner during the trial doing her no favours. Aged 22 at her execution, she remains the youngest woman to die judicially under British law in the twentieth century.

It was with this woman that Hellinger had to work. This was a difficult negotiation. As Hellinger wrote in her memoir, Grese was evil, but also "vulnerable and impressionable" and subject to manipulation. Hellinger manipulated her as best she could. It was a small mercy, but it is said that Grese whipped prisoners only when Hellinger wasn't around to watch. If Hellinger was there she felt ashamed to do so.

Put first in charge of the French and Polish women, Hellinger did what she could to bring comfort, and to explain to newcomers the rules – official and unofficial – of camp life. If there were secret ways to survive, Hellinger told them – in the camps, new techniques were constantly being shared among the inmates.

She was also put in charge of the block that housed women who were undergoing medical experiments, often around sterilization – part of the Final Solution was to stop Jews breeding, often excruciating, always humiliating.

Hellinger tried as best she could to comfort these women, whose trauma on each day was only exacerbated by the knowledge that the trauma would continue the next day. And usually until they were dead. According to her memoir, the only thing that could be done was to try and fill the minds of the women with something other than what they were going through. "How could I make this inescapable hell just a little less hellish?" she says she asked herself.

So she told them stories, and organized full cabaret shows, with everyone taking a role, rehearsing, performing. The shows made oblique, and sometimes not so oblique,

THE ELDER

references to their Nazi captors. They found a freedom in laughing at the sad men and women who wished to be the master race.

Finally, Magda was made camp elder of Birkenau's Camp C, where she coordinated food distribution and hygiene for 30,000 female prisoners. She continued to try and boost morale, but she also carried out practical and often bald-faced interventions into camp life. She would unashamedly lead some girls away from the queue on the left to the gas chambers to the queue on the right. Once she even found out that a barrack of 800 girls "no older than 16" were supposed to be gassed the next day. She managed to get 400 of them out to hide – not everyone, but still 400 souls. The chaotic administration of the camps meant that the girls had missed their turn, and that was that. One of the SS guards once said to her, "For a Jew, you have indeed got something in your head."

Another time, Hellinger discovered many women had been selected to go to the gas chambers and were being held in Block 25 the night before their death. So, during the night, she got the guard on the door drunk. He fell asleep and she was able to let the women out of the block 100 at a time, giving them refuge until they were relocated to their own blocks.

She was not afraid to make demands of the guards either. Arriving at one barracks, she complained to the commander that there were no beds, mattresses or blankets. She called the commander a coward for not being strong enough to demand them. The next day the women got their beds and bedding.

STORIES OF HOPE FROM AUSCHWITZ

By protecting others, she was sometimes protected herself. Falling sick with typhus generally meant the gas chamber, but when she got it, guards and inmates protected her from selection. When she spent time in a standing cell – a 90-by-90-centimetre (35-by-35-inch) room with four women in the small space, standing all night – and could not sleep, but was still expected, as all inmates, to do her work assignments, others pitched in. And once when she was being loaded onto a truck to be gassed, a guard stepped in and pulled her away.

During the forced march out of Auschwitz, Magda was rescued by partisans. After first returning to Czechoslovakia, Magda immigrated to Israel. She later moved to Australia and wrote her memoir with her daughter, Maya.

Maya's father was a man named Blau. Born in 1910, in Bratislava, Slovakia, at age 16 Blau began working as a salesman for a textile business. In 1930 he was called up for 18 months of army service. He married and had a son in 1937. Evicted from their house in March 1939, the family was sent to Auschwitz – he was selected for work duties; his wife and son were sent to the gas chambers.

He did forced labour at the camp for four years. One day a drunk guard told him there was a woman he thought he might like to meet, Magda Hellinger. They fell in love. But as the camp was being eradicated, they were sent on different death marches. Magda asked him how they would find each other again if they survived. Blau said, "My number is 65066 and yours 2318. $6 + 5 = 11$, $6 + 6 = 12$, $11 + 12 = 23$, and $6 \times 3 = 18$. Simple as that." She just had to do the sum to remember. She did – they found each other and were married.

THE ELDER

Did Magda Hellinger have to do her work in a grey zone, making moral decisions she would not have made in normal life? Undoubtedly. But did her moral choices save lives and bring comfort and hope? Yes, they did.

THE PRISONER REVOLT

One of the myths of Auschwitz is that resistance was useless. As we have seen, there were hundreds of tiny acts of resistance every day, from sharing food to offering prayers. But there were also outstanding acts carried out by those who had nothing but found ways to strike back against those who would destroy them.

On 7 October 1944, a fire broke out in crematorium IV. This was no accident. For the last few months four extraordinary women, Regina Safirsztajn, Estera Wajcblum, Ala Gertner and Róża Robota, had been smuggling gunpowder into the camp. This was for a growing Polish resistance movement in Auschwitz. Other members of the resistance were able to communicate with the Polish underground outside and were able to gradually and surreptitiously make weapons.

The main protagonists were members of the Auschwitz Sonderkommando, prisoners, usually Jews, who were forced to help with the disposal of gas chamber victims. For a year they had been planning an uprising. To the frustration of the Sonderkommando, the Polish underground outside urged delays, as they argued that it was best to wait until the approaching Soviet army was closer.

But on 7 October rumours spread that the camp commandants were suspicious. One of the resistance leaders was interrogated and shot. It was believed that the rest of the Sonderkommando was to be killed the next day. It was decided to initiate the uprising.

The fire was set. Members of the Sonderkommando charged at guards with iron poles and knives, beating them and leaving three dead. Other prisoners ran to the fence and cut the wire so that they could escape.

As news of the revolt spread, other camp inmates grabbed weapons from their guards and attacked. Two more SS men were shot, and others were thrown into the burning crematorium. More men fled through the gap in the fence, making it as far as a granary 5 kilometres (3 miles) away.

But the revolt was to fail. The Nazis found the granary and burned it down, killing everyone inside. The four women who had smuggled in the gunpowder were tortured but would not offer any information on how they had done it. They were hanged in front of the other prisoners, but as they placed the noose around Róża Robota's neck, she cried out, "Sisters, revenge!"

In all, 250 prisoners died in the uprising and in the reprisals. Is there hope in this? For those who witnessed the uprising, there was no doubt. The mere fact of such a bold, audacious and clever act showed that those on the side of justice could organize a way to defeat their oppressors. And it also showed that there were more and more holes in the Nazi armour. There was no way such an uprising could have even been started a year earlier.

THE PRISONER REVOLT

Sometimes the greatest victories can look like defeat. For those who died as part of the revolt, such as Regina Safirsztajn, Estera Wajcblum, Ala Gertner and Róża Robota, there would be no final deliverance from Auschwitz back to their lives and their families. But for those who they inspired – "Sisters, revenge" – every day that they lived in the camp after the revolt was a vindication of their struggle.

THE DOCTOR AND HER ASSISTANT

She could hear the sound of trumpets, cheering, British voices. There was jubilation. The atmosphere, oppressive so long, suddenly seemed to lift. Liberation had arrived.

But Gisella Perl was busy. She was with a young Polish woman named Marusa, and Marusa was giving birth. It was one of hundreds of pregnancies that she had dealt with at Auschwitz. But this time she was going to do something she had not been able to do before. She was going to try and save the baby's life, rather than kill it.

Gisella Perl was born in 1907 in Sighet, then part of Hungary, also the birthplace of Elie Wiesel (see page 149). In 1923, at age 16, she graduated first in her secondary school class – the only woman and the only Jew. Her father had initially told her not to study medicine, thinking it would make her lose her faith. She was the eldest of seven children in an Orthodox family; the children studied the Torah for hours every day, and singing filled the home every Friday evening for Shabbat.

But she persisted and her father relented after she made

a vow over a prayer book he had given to her. "I swear on this book… I shall always remain a good, true Jew." Years later, when she had patients of her own, she would buy him another prayer book, engraved with his name. As she later said in her memoir, he would carry it with him to the gas chambers at Auschwitz.

Gisella was a brilliant student and would become a brilliant doctor. In fact, all of the children were intellectuals and all but one would receive doctorates in medicine and other fields. She also spoke many languages, including Hungarian, Romanian, German, French and Yiddish. This would be crucial in her later life.

On graduation, Gisella started working at the local hospital as a gynaecologist – she was always most interested in looking after women and loved bringing babies into the world. She married Ephraim Krauss and seemed set for a long and successful career, with the added bonus that came with her area of work – seeing the children she delivered grow up and have their own children.

Then Hungary fell to the Nazis. Perl and most of her family were rounded up and sent to the crowded Sighet ghetto and then to Auschwitz – a few of the 400,000 Jews sent to Auschwitz that year. Her own daughter, Gabriella, was hidden away with a non-Jewish family, but Perl had no way of knowing she was safe – every child she saw and baby she delivered must have broken her heart. Her son came with her to the camp.

Arriving at the camp, she and her husband were separated, but they made a vow to each other: "We will meet someday in Jerusalem."

THE DOCTOR AND HER ASSISTANT

When Josef Mengele found out she was a gynaecologist, Gisella was ordered, with four other doctors and four nurses, to set up a hospital in the camp. This was, of course, no ordinary hospital. Its primary purpose was not to heal the sick, but to carry out experiments on the healthy. She had brought her medical kit with her, but it was taken away. One of the German doctors on site told her she was going to be the camp gynaecologist. He said, "Don't worry about instruments... you won't have any."

And so it was. Perl provided as much medical help as she could to the women in her care. She was often called on to perform general medical procedures which required drugs, sterile conditions and basic medical equipment – but despite these being available to doctors like Mengele, she had to work without. Removing infected teeth. Bandaging wounds. Seeing to inmates with broken bones – ribs, jaws, arms. Often these were injuries directly caused by camp guards, such as the notorious Irma Grese.

Perl wrote in her memoir *I Was a Doctor in Auschwitz* that the work filled her with "impotent distress", but those she tended to and who survived were in no doubt that they owed their lives to her. One inmate was cured of blindness when she managed to procure some vitamins to inject into him. She also often offered up vials of her own blood as substitutes for those of inmates suspected of having diseases – having a disease meant an immediate transfer to the gas chamber.

But it was in her role as gynaecologist that her work became both heroic and tragic.

She was told by Mengele to let him know of any woman

who was pregnant. He told her they would be sent to a special camp, where they would receive extra bread rations and even milk. But she soon found this was a lie, after seeing a group of pregnant women beaten and thrown, alive, into a fire. The Final Solution wanted no more Jewish children – many of the medical experiments at the camp were aimed at finding ways to sterilize women. Those who were pregnant had to be killed.

Perl made a decision that was absolutely momentous. She would take it upon herself to kill the unborn children in order to save their mothers.

This was of course against everything she believed as a doctor, as a religious Jew, and as a human being. But if the authorities found out a woman was pregnant, they would kill both the woman and the child. By killing the child, Perl would let the woman live, and maybe after the hell of Auschwitz the woman would be able to produce another child who could live and prosper.

Women who found out they were pregnant were referred to her immediately by the camp elder in charge of their block. Perl would then explain the situation to them. If the child was born, then both would be killed, and if anyone found out before the child was born, they would be beaten to death. The baby needed to be aborted – the death of the child would save the mother.

Perl took the pregnant women to the hospital in the middle of the night and performed the abortion, sometimes later into the term than was ideal. And, as ever, she had no medical equipment, and no anaesthetic. The chances of infection were high. The women also had to keep as quiet

THE DOCTOR AND HER ASSISTANT

as possible even as they went through the agony, and they knew that the next day they would have to carry out their hard labour without flinching, so as not to alert the guards to their condition and be gassed.

Perl had an assistant in her work, 17-year-old Lea Fridler, whose main job was to hold a candle so that the gynaecologist could see what she was doing. Fridler had arrived on the same train as Perl – her number was A-25402, and Perl's was A-25404.

Fridler was born in Oradea, in what is now Romania, in 1927 and was, she said, a spoiled child. But she suffered the same upheavals as all the Jews in Europe under Nazi dictatorship, and at 16 she was taken to Auschwitz in a train. Her mother, a nurse, was also taken, and assigned to Mengele's hospital. Lea was also given work there, doing odd jobs. This would come to include assisting Dr Perl in carrying out her secret, life-saving abortions.

Talking to the *Jerusalem Post* in 2013, the 85-year-old Fridler described Mengele's initial discussions with Perl – he said he wanted to get hold of women in the early stages of pregnancy and experiment on their babies. This soon became too much to organize, so instead he chose to kill them. Fridler did however see one baby brought to term. Mengele left it with the mother for a month before deciding it was too difficult having it at the camp. It was killed by being thrown on the floor.

Meanwhile, Perl remembered being forced to deliver a set of twins for Mengele, who would carry out experiments on one and compare the results against the other. She never saw the twins again. He also had her extract an eight-week-old foetus from a pregnant woman and preserve it in a glass jar so it could be sent to Berlin.

One baby boy brought to term particularly upset her. He belonged to a woman named Yolanda, from Perl's hometown of Sighet. Having taught herself to act quickly and definitively with newborns, Perl found she just could not kill this little one. For two days she hid him, but his cries were likely to attract attention soon. So she had to act. She later said she kissed him once and then had to strangle him, before adding his body to a pile of corpses awaiting cremation.

In March 1945, as Auschwitz closed, both Perl and Fridler were transferred by death march to Bergen-Belsen. There they continued their work, carrying out nightly abortions at huge personal risk. It was there that Perl heard the trumpets of liberation, while delivering Marusa's baby. This one, she was determined, would survive.

But soon after birth, the baby's face and lips grew pale. Blood came out between Marusa's legs. When this had happened before, Perl could only watch the baby die. But she wasn't going to do the same this time. She ran into the yard, found a British soldier, and was given access to surgical equipment, water and antiseptic, none of which had been available to her before in her time at the camps. She had water, she had disinfectant, and she saved the mother and child. She was, she would later say, back to saving lives, not having to end them.

As inmates of Bergen-Belsen were repatriated, Perl stayed on, delivering more babies, giving the gift of life. By the time she left, official repatriation had almost ceased, and she spent 19 days walking around Germany looking for her family. But tragedy was to follow – she learned that her husband had been beaten to death by the SS shortly before the liberation. And her beloved son had been burned alive.

It was too much. All of those babies, all of that death – she had managed to block it out. But to know that her husband and son were dead, and had died horribly, was, for her, the final straw. Dr Gisella Perl, who had saved so many by taking lives, tried to take her own with poison. But this time she failed. This was rock bottom, and now she began to climb out.

She made it home and was reunited with her daughter Gabriella, who had been kept safe. She decided to speak out – she didn't want to be a doctor, she wanted to be a witness. She was invited to the White House by Eleanor Roosevelt and had US citizenship fast-tracked. She also wrote to the US War Department to offer herself up as a witness at any trial of Mengele. He was, she said, the most perverse mass murderer of the twentieth century. She also gave evidence against Irma Grese, which saw her executed.

Gisella went back to medicine, working at the Mount Sinai Hospital in Manhattan and then opening her own practice, while publishing academic papers on women's reproductive health. Finally, she moved to Israel in 1978 and was welcomed as a hero. Her grandson witnessed people literally falling at her feet.

Lea Fridler and her mother were both sent on a death march as Auschwitz closed. Lea remembered a time when she was so sad and ashamed she could no longer eat, but her mother got angry at her and forced her to. Her life was saved, she said, by her mother. Fridler failed to mention the lives she had saved too.

When the two of them arrived home on 11 May 1945, there were no friends or family there to greet them – they were all dead, including Lea's father. The pair headed back to find their old house, and as they did so, a man rushed up to Lea, grabbed her and said, "Thank God you are alive! You came back! How are you?" His name was Yossi, they had been to school together – and soon after they were married. They had two children, 22 grandchildren and 44 great-grandchildren – and counting.

There is a famous video clip of the British humanitarian Sir Nicholas Winton, who rescued 669 children from Czechoslovakia on the eve of World War Two. Winton is in a TV studio full of people, and the host asks everyone who owes their life to him to stand up. One by one, everyone stands.

Imagine how many would stand if the same question were asked about Dr Gisella Perl and Lea Fridler.

BOOKS DON'T DIE

Her daughter kept it for 50 years, thinking it was a diary and that it would be too painful to read. Denise Epstein could not face reading what her mother Irène Némirovsky went through during the Holocaust, where she was to die at the age of 39. So she kept the small journal hidden away and got on with her life.

It was not until 2002 that she opened it and read what was to become an international bestseller, her mother's novel, *Suite Française*.

Irina Lvovna Nemirovskaya was born in 1903 in Kyiv in Ukraine, which was then part of Russia. When the Soviets came to power in 1917, the family fled to Finland and later Paris. Her father, a wealthy banker, re-established himself there, while his daughter attended the Sorbonne and began writing when she was 18 years old. In 1929, she published *David Golder*, the story of a Jewish banker unable to please his troubled daughter, drawn from her own life. It was a success and became a film.

Meanwhile, she married Michael Epstein, a banker, and had two daughters: Denise, born in 1929, and Élisabeth (Babet) in 1937. Her attempts to become a French citizen failed, despite her renown as an author. In 1939, she converted to Catholicism and seemed to be settling down to a successful life in Paris.

But then the Nazis overran her adopted homeland. By 1940, Némirovsky's husband was unable to continue working at the bank, and her books could no longer be published, because of her Jewish ancestry. Under Nazi racial laws, her conversion to Catholicism meant nothing.

Fleeing the capital, Némirovsky, her husband and children ended up in the village of Issy-l'Évêque. She continued to write, and it was here that she began working on what Denise thought was a journal. The family had hoped to escape the Nazis, but on 13 July 1942 Némirovsky was arrested in front of her daughters as a "stateless person of Jewish descent" by policemen employed by Vichy France. She was 39 years old. She would not make it to 40.

As she was being taken away, she told her daughters, "I am going on a journey now." They would never see her again.

She was first taken to a convoy assembly camp at Pithiviers, and on 17 July 1942, together with 928 other Jewish deportees, transported to Auschwitz. There she went through the humiliation meted out to all new arrivals, having her head shaved and her forearm tattooed. She was not sent to the gas chamber, as she was still regarded as capable of work, and so began hard labour. But soon after, she contracted typhus and died on 17 August 1942. A few months later Michael Epstein was also arrested and sent to Auschwitz. He went immediately to the gas chamber, dying on 6 November 1942.

BOOKS DON'T DIE

After their parents were arrested, the children were detained, but according to Denise's later testimony, she reminded the arresting officer of his own daughter, and he let the two girls go. The girls were hidden for the duration of the war by a French woman whom Némirovsky had employed as a nanny and who had become a friend of the family. They would remember going to the train station every day after the liberation to see if their parents returned – they wore placards around their necks on which they had written the family name. Each day they were disappointed.

After the war, Denise Epstein worked as an archivist, eventually settling in Toulouse, and her younger sister Babet – now Élisabeth Gille – became a noted editor and translator. Their mother's books were out of print, but Élisabeth wrote a series of memoirs about her mother, which were published to some acclaim. She died in 2002.

Denise still had in her possession a battered suitcase that contained papers belonging to their mother. She could not bring herself to open it. But on the death of her sister she decided it was time to open the suitcase and read the manuscript. It was written in tiny handwriting and she needed a magnifying glass to read it. It was not a journal but a novel, chronicling life in France before and during the Nazi occupation. Planned as a sequence of five novels – Némirovsky had plotted out the rest – the manuscript was the first two books. Denise sent them to a publisher and they were published as one volume in 2004 under the name *Suite Française* (*French Suite*).

The book was received with acclaim. *The New York Times* called the book "stunning" and argued that it ranks with "the greatest, most humane and incisive fiction that conflict has produced". It was soon adapted as a film. It spent two years on *The Times*' bestseller list, bringing the conflict to a whole new readership. Her earlier novels were republished too, again to acclaim.

For Denise, the success of the book was both a shock and a confirmation of her mother's talent. But it also brought back the woman herself, who, for all that the Nazis tried to turn her into a number, and for all that the Nazis eventually turned her into a victim, has outlived them by many years, and will outlive them for many more. Another triumph of hope.

THE FUGITIVE

They say there is a law of unintended consequences. But it seems that kindness almost always brings consequences that are good.

Austrian-born Freddie Knoller was 21 when – after several years of living with false identities, and being part of the resistance – he was placed on a train to Auschwitz, one of the infamous cattle cars, without food or water, and horrendously overcrowded. Beside him was a Frenchman called Robert, who was much older than Freddie. Freddie took it upon himself to look after Robert, protecting him as best he could despite their language differences.

When they left the train at Auschwitz, that might have been it. What Freddie didn't know was that Robert was a doctor and the SS would put him in charge of the camp hospital barracks, which meant he was given extra rations – which he then shared with Freddie. It was these extra rations, Freddie always said, that kept him alive. Robert also helped transfer Freddie to a friend's work unit.

Freddie's had been an extraordinary life in extraordinary circumstances, even before he arrived in Auschwitz. He was born in Vienna on 17 April 1921 and had two brothers,

Erich and Otto. The three of them performed music together, Freddie on the cello, calling themselves "The Knoller Brothers Trio".

While anti-Semitism was ever-present, it wasn't until 1938, when the Anschluss joined Germany and Austria together, that the attacks became constant and physical. He and his brothers left Vienna – his parents decided that in their fifties they would be safe from persecution, only to be rounded up and taken to the concentration camp at Theresienstadt and then on to Auschwitz.

The brothers each went their separate ways – Erich to the US, Otto to Holland and Freddie to Belgium, where he found refuge with the Jewish community in Antwerp at a refugee camp in Merksplas and then later at another in Eksaarde, where he joined the orchestra. But then Germany invaded Belgium in May 1940, and Freddie Knoller found himself on the run again.

He made it as far as the French border before being arrested. He was held in Saint-Cyprien internment camp, but managed to escape and run 10 kilometres (6 miles) to the border of unoccupied France, where he sought refuge with his aunt and uncle in Gaillac. But he became bored and decided to head to Paris.

There, he assumed a false name, Robert Metz, and pretended he was not Jewish – which was particularly important as he found a job procuring women for Gestapo officers in the red light district. He would later tell of one close shave, when a Gestapo officer told him he could tell who was Jewish by measuring the circumference of their head. He measured Freddie's head and Freddie passed the test.

THE FUGITIVE

But in 1943 his luck ran out. Having left Paris for southern France, he was betrayed to the Gestapo by a jilted lover. Tortured, he confessed to being Jewish. He was taken to Drancy for processing and then placed in a cattle car. He did not know it at the time but he had already met his saviour, the French doctor Robert.

Freddie spent all of 1944 in back-breaking labour in Auschwitz, seeing many of those he worked with give up and die. In January 1945, the Russians were advancing towards Auschwitz and the Nazis decided to empty the camp. The death march began, eventually reaching a new camp, Mittelbau-Dora, where the manufacture of rockets continued. Working conditions were as brutal as at Auschwitz – around one in three of the roughly 60,000 prisoners who were sent to the camp died. Freddie was finally liberated in April 1945.

Once back in France, Freddie Knoller was reunited with his brother Erich, who had become a soldier in the US Army. In 1947 Freddie emigrated to the US, where he met and married his British wife Freda, and the couple moved to the UK in 1952.

But who was Robert, the French doctor who Freddie helped, and who helped him? His story, as we shall see on the next page, is also one of hope and survival.

THE SAVIOUR

He was born in Neuvy, France, on 20 May 1900, and moved to Paris after high school to study medicine, receiving his degree in 1931. In 1933, he became an associate professor at the Université de Strasbourg. Dr Robert Waitz was a man dedicated to his profession – helping the sick and injured. He could not have guessed what that work would require of him.

When France surrendered to Germany in 1940, Waitz joined the resistance, rising to the head of one of the main divisions.

It was in this capacity that he was arrested by the Gestapo on 3 July 1943. After a time in prison in Moulins, he was placed in a cattle car to go to Auschwitz. It was there he met Freddie Knoller and others who would remember him later for trying to keep their spirits up.

At Auschwitz Waitz was employed as physician for the in-house clinic in the camp's prisoner infirmary. With access to only a small quantity of aspirin and some charcoal, he tended to inmates suffering from malnutrition and fatigue, and to those who had endured torture. His patients were particularly moved by the time he would take over them

– asking lots of questions. It was one of the few times in the camp that they felt they were being treated as a human being, rather than a number.

He was often called upon to decide which inmates were too sick to work and would therefore qualify for the gas chamber. His answer was always the same – each individual was perfectly capable of work, they just needed a little rest.

A colleague and fellow survivor, Leon Stasiak, said of Waitz that it sometimes seemed that he had simply refused to acknowledge that he was operating in a concentration camp – he acted in exactly the same way as if he was at a major hospital, with access to equipment and medicine. His consultations were as long and as thorough as they would have been outside the camp, and he had no interest in the efforts of the SS guards to hurry him along. After his shifts he would move about the camp, often visiting the young and vulnerable to give them any spare food or medicine he had to hand and again asking them questions to ascertain if there was anything he could do.

There was, thought Stasiak, a second possible reason for Waitz's thoroughness – he was carrying out his own research into the condition of the inmates, with a view to providing evidence when the Nazis lost, as he was sure they would. He had been a resistance fighter outside the camp; he would continue the fight within, by whatever means necessary.

This involved tremendous risks – he often overruled SS commands to release an inmate from the sick bay, allowing them to spend longer recuperating and daring the guards to stop him. Once, he saved a Soviet pilot from being taken to his certain death by giving him an injection which raised

THE SAVIOUR

his temperature sufficiently for him to miss the transport he was to be put on.

Another time, when an Allied raid dropped bombs near the camp, Stasiak was astonished to see Waitz, known for his lack of concern during other raids, go down on all fours as though in fear. It later transpired that he had grabbed an expensive microscope, an invaluable piece of equipment, placed it on the floor and crouched over it to stop it being destroyed. He was embarrassed that he had been seen doing this.

On the death march from Auschwitz in January 1945, Waitz was forced to walk to Gleiwitz, and was then transported in an open cattle car to Buchenwald. During the march, he continued to treat inmates, again taking his time, even if it delayed things. He still held on to the same two convictions – that the best form of resistance was to do his job, and that the Nazis would lose.

They did, and as soon as he was liberated he started the task of publishing his findings. As early as 1947, he published an account of his time and work in the prisoner infirmary. He also served as chairman of the International Auschwitz Committee for several years. He passed away in 1978 after a long and successful career as a physician.

Long after the war, Freddie Knoller searched for Dr Waitz and tracked him down to the centre of Paris. He found his house and Dr Waitz's wife opened the door. She asked Freddie in and told him her husband had died a few months earlier. Freddie told her that he owed him his life.

There are surely many others who owed their life after the war to Dr Robert Waitz.

THE AUSCHWITZ BABY

The Russians were coming – everyone in Auschwitz knew that in November 1944. The camp was gradually going to pieces, conditions were becoming even worse, not only for the inmates but for those guarding them. They all knew that the Soviet army would be there soon, and for those incarcerated, the trick was to try and stay alive until they got there.

Among the decisions taken by the camp authorities was to shut down the gas chambers, in part because they were running out of money, but also in preparation for trying to deny that the chambers ever existed. New arrivals at the camp would no longer go through the selection process. There would be no more exterminations.

The order to make this change was given on 1 November. The next day two-year-old Eva Umlauf arrived at the camp with her mother Agnes. Had they arrived two days earlier they would have gone straight to the gas chamber. Not only because Eva was so little, but because Agnes was four months pregnant. On 30 October, 18,000 mothers and children who had arrived from Theresienstadt were killed.

Despite her age, Eva received her tattoo, prisoner A-26959. Later she would be haunted by the question of why it was necessary. "Why did they choose to tattoo a two-year-old baby?" she asked. The only answer she could find is that, to her guards, the prisoners were subhuman, whether they were two years old or 80 years old.

Eva and Agnes's stay in Auschwitz was traumatic but thankfully short. On 27 January, the Soviets arrived and liberated the camp. But her time there had left little Eva very sick, and she was kept in the camp infirmary. Her mother was told that her daughter was not expected to survive, but she was having none of it. She did everything in her power to keep her daughter alive, and she succeeded.

But Agnes was also suffering – she was diagnosed with rickets, TB and jaundice. She too was held in the Auschwitz infirmary, where doctors cared for her as best they could. The chances that she would be able to deliver her baby were almost zero. Almost. In April 1945, Agnes gave birth to her new daughter, Leonore – a miracle baby born from the ashes of Auschwitz which, as Eva puts it, shows that even in the darkest place on earth, with all its atrocities, you can still create a new life and new beginnings.

Of course, nothing could ever completely replace what had been lost – Agnes had lost her family, her husband, her father, mother and three siblings, her grandparents and great-grandparents, as well as the family's fortune. But as Eva relates, Agnes tried to give her girls as normal a life as possible.

Eva herself left the Communist regime in Czechoslovakia in 1967 and moved to West Germany, where she had three children. The little girl the Nazis tried to turn into prisoner A-26959 became a paediatrician and psychotherapist, treating thousands of children throughout her medical career, and creating a beautiful family of her own.

DANDELION

It is almost impossibly moving. There are nine people prominent in the photograph, sitting on the grass in a circle, with others standing in the background.

On the far left of the photograph is a woman in a black headscarf, facing away from the camera. To her left in the circle, a woman in a white headscarf, tied at the back, also facing away, though you can see the bottom half of her face. Behind her, a boy of four or five, in a cap and a jacket, his back to the camera. Then, on the far side of the circle, another woman, facing us, but looking at a child. She is squinting in the sun.

To her left, a boy of seven or eight, also facing us. He too is wearing a cap and jacket, and on his chest is a star – the photograph is black and white, but the star is undoubtedly yellow. Beside him another, younger boy, perhaps his brother, his cap pushed back on his high forehead. He holds his hands together, maybe clapping, maybe keeping in the fidgets that afflict four-year-old boys.

Then in the foreground of the picture, an older boy, perhaps ten, taking up the front right of the photograph with his mouth open as though speaking, and next to him a small girl, maybe his sister, her hair neatly parted, mouth also open because brothers and sisters talk at the same time.

And finally, just to the left of the centre of the photograph, and part of the circle, a small child, no older than two. She is swathed in a cardigan. This is a picture from spring, surely – it is definitely sunny, but everyone is in layers. Her right hand is raised to the women and children on the other side of the photograph. She is holding up a dandelion she has just found, and in her excitement she wants to show it to everyone. Look, everyone, look.

It looks like a beautiful day out, all these people gathered on the grass. But they are all waiting outside the Auschwitz gas chambers. Within an hour of them being photographed, everyone in this picture will be dead.

One way to read this picture is to decide that all beautiful human gestures, a small child holding a dandelion, are destined for destruction when they meet a force as evil as the Nazis. But stop, and reverse. The Nazis are gone. Little girls still pick dandelions and hold them up to show people, because they are so, so excited.

So which is stronger?

THE BANKNOTE

It said simply this: "A start to a new life... good luck and happiness."

It was April 1945, and 21-year-old Lily Ebert had just been liberated from Auschwitz by a battalion of US troops – a day she had thought many times would never come. As the soldiers moved around the camp, shocked by what they saw, giving assistance where they could, one of them told Lily he wanted to write something down for her, some words he was feeling needed to be said.

He searched for a piece of paper but could find nothing. Instead he took from his wallet a German Reichsmark and wrote around the edges that simple message of hope. He gave it to her and went back to work.

Lily Ebert was born in 1923 in a comfortably well-off family in Bonyhád, Hungary, the oldest daughter of six children. She would later describe her parents as the best parents possible. Her childhood was a happy one, until Adolf Hitler came to power in Germany, the war began and, in March 1944, Hungary was occupied. Falling under Nazi rule meant any Jew, secular or religious, was vulnerable.

STORIES OF HOPE FROM AUSCHWITZ

It didn't take long. In July Lily, her mother Nina, younger brother Bela and three sisters Berta, Renee and Piri were deported to Auschwitz-Birkenau. Her older brother was sent to another camp. At the selection on arrival, Nina, Bela and Berta were sent to the left, while Lily and her two other sisters were sent to the right. The left was the gas chambers, and Lily never saw her mother, brother or sister again.

Lily and her two sisters were selected for work, first in the camp, and then four months later in a munitions factory. There they worked in appalling conditions, on meagre rations and facing brutal punishment if they slowed down. And always the threat of the gas chamber for anyone who ceased to be useful.

Then came April 1945, the camp suddenly empty of German soldiers, and the arrival of the US soldiers. Later Lily would remind people that those who were in Auschwitz owned literally nothing, only the clothes they were wearing when the camp was liberated. And now Lily had a banknote, worthless in monetary terms but priceless in meaning. She kept it. And 70 years passed.

One day she told her great-grandson Dov Forman about the banknote. Dov was one of 38 great-grandchildren – Lily and her surviving sisters had emigrated to Switzerland, and later Lily went on to Israel, where she married and had three children. She and her family then emigrated to Britain in 1967.

Dov posted the note on his social media accounts and left his phone for a few hours. When he looked at it again, it had 8,000 hits and growing. Soon it was shared by the

THE BANKNOTE

Auschwitz-Birkenau Museum to its 1 million followers, and the number of hits went into the millions. Within 24 hours the soldier had been identified.

Private Hayman Shulman was from Brooklyn and had been inducted into the US Army in 1942. He was immediately sent to Europe and was not only at the liberation of Auschwitz but also of Buchenwald. He worked as an aide to Rabbi Herschel Schacter, the first Jewish chaplain to enter Buchenwald, who would help resettle displaced persons from the camp, including Elie Wiesel (see page 149).

Hayman wrote to his wife Sandy every day, in code to avoid military censorship. These letters were factual but also emotional, making him not only a witness to history, but also an accidental participant, as Sandy told *The New York Times* in 2015. Of Buchenwald he wrote that the stench from the many dead bodies was nothing compared to the sight they presented. It is a description which might equally have applied to Auschwitz.

After the war, Hayman went into the jewellery business and performed as a singer under the name Howard Shaw. He rarely talked about what he had seen during the war, although his son Jason often asked him. "He wouldn't talk about it ever. I had to pry it out of him," he said.

Hayman died in 2013, before Lily and Dov identified him, but in July 2020, they had an online meeting with his family. Lily said to Jason, "Your father showed me that there was good in humanity and gave me hope for a better future."

And she added, "I am overwhelmed that my great-grandson has been able to reunite me with Private Shulman's family. It is the ultimate proof that the Nazis did not win."

STORIES OF HOPE FROM AUSCHWITZ

In 2021, Lily and Dov co-authored a book about her experiences, *Lily's Promise: How I Survived Auschwitz and Found the Strength to Live*, with a foreword by the then Prince Charles. It was one of Waterstones' best history books of 2021. Lily also revisited Auschwitz and had a word to say to the camp: "You are not alive any more. And I am here."

Prince Charles also commissioned Lily's portrait as one of seven for the Royal Collection to remember survivors of the Holocaust. When she went to Buckingham Palace for the unveiling, she said to Prince Charles, "Meeting you, it is for everyone who lost their lives." Prince Charles touched her shoulder and replied, "But it is a greater privilege for me."

THE PRIEST

July 1941. The early days of the camp. No one knows how, but three men had escaped from Auschwitz. Everyone knew reprisals would be swift. They were. The deputy commander of Auschwitz ordered ten men to be chosen at random to be starved to death in an underground bunker. One man was Franciszek Gajowniczek. As he was selected he cried out, "My wife! My children!"

Watching was a man named Maximilian Kolbe. What he did next not only became a symbol of love, bravery and resistance, it would also see him made a saint in the Catholic Church by Pope John Paul II in 1982. Kolbe stepped forward from those watching and said, "I am a priest; I want to die for him!"

Maximilian Kolbe was born on 8 January 1894 in Zduńska Wola, in the Kingdom of Poland, which was then part of the Russian Empire. His father was a weaver, and his mother was a midwife. His birth name was Raymund, but he changed it to Maximilian for religious reasons.

When he was nine, one of the moments that would shape his life took place – he had a vision of the Virgin Mary, who came to him holding a white and a red crown.

She asked him whether he was willing to accept either of them. "The white one meant that I should persevere in purity and the red that I should become a martyr. I said that I would accept them both."

Aged 13, he joined the Franciscan seminary. During his studies, World War One broke out, and the second life-shaping event occurred. His father chose not to fight with Poland's Russian rulers, but with the Polish legions fighting for his country's independence. He was caught and hanged as a traitor by the Russians.

Kolbe was ordained as a priest in 1918 and, after completing his studies, returned to the newly independent Poland in 1919. He settled in the monastery of Niepokalanów near Warsaw. He caught tuberculosis and would be affected by it for the rest of his life, but he always said he was "suffering for the Virgin Mary".

In 1930 Kolbe travelled to Japan and set up a monastery in Nagasaki. When the atomic bomb was dropped in 1945, the monastery was shielded by a mountain. It was one of the few places left standing and remains in operation. But Kolbe's illness brought him back to Poland.

At the time of the German invasion, Kolbe was working at his monastery in Niepokalanów. He was arrested in September 1939 and spent two months in prison. He was offered and declined the opportunity to declare himself of German ancestry by signing the document called the Deutsche Volksliste. He turned part of his monastery into a publishing house and started to produce anti-Nazi texts.

On 17 February 1941, the monastery was shut down by the German authorities, and Kolbe was arrested. He

THE PRIEST

was sent to Pawiak prison, and then on 28 May to a new concentration camp, called Auschwitz.

There he met another Polish Catholic, Franciszek Gajowniczek. Gajowniczek was born in a small village in 1901 and moved to the capital Warsaw in 1921. There he married a woman named Helena and had two sons, Bogdan, born in 1927, and Juliusz, born in 1930. A professional soldier, he fought to defend Poland against the Nazis in 1939 and was captured during the Battle of Modin. He was taken to a forced labour camp in a place called Tarnów. On 8 October 1940, after enduring seven months of brutal interrogation, he was transferred to Auschwitz, where he became prisoner number 5659.

He and Kolbe, prisoner number 16670, met in early 1941. Auschwitz at the time had not reached the level of brutality that occurred later. It was much more like a standard prisoner-of-war camp, and the prisoners were able to mingle sometimes. Gajowniczek and Kolbe were not close, but as Catholic Poles they did encounter each other on occasion.

Then three men escaped.

When the random selection was made and Gajowniczek was chosen, many prisoners witnessed what happened next. There was a stunned silence when Kolbe spoke up. It is, of course, impossible to put ourselves into the shoes of the other men there. Did they feel guilt they had not done the same? Shame? Did they feel, after all they had been through, nothing? Or did they feel hope, seeing such a display of humanity? Kolbe must have hoped the latter.

Kolbe and the other nine men were led away to a prison cell. There they stayed for two weeks without food or water.

Each time a guard checked on them they were confronted with the same sight; Kolbe standing or kneeling calmly, sometimes in prayer. He did not take his eyes off the guard.

After those two weeks, of the ten men, only four were still alive, one of whom was Maximilian Kolbe – the others lay there as corpses. The guards wanted the bunker emptied, so on 14 August, they gave the four remaining prisoners lethal injections of carbolic acid. Kolbe is said to have raised his left arm and calmly waited for the syringe. Again he stared into the eyes of his guard, his executioner.

What did Gajowniczek feel during this time? As he told it later, he felt a sense of hope and of duty. When in 1942 he contracted typhus, but, with the assistance of fellow prisoners, fought it off, he said that he wanted to live so that Father Kolbe's sacrifice "wouldn't be in vain", and that he had given him strength. "How could I waste his life? He offered it so I could live with my wife and enjoy my sons."

Gajowniczek was transferred from Auschwitz to Sachsenhausen concentration camp on 25 October 1944. He survived a death march two weeks before the war's end – 12 days without food or water, subsisting on nettles and dry grass. Finally, in late 1945, after another five months and nine days in concentration camps, he was united with Helena.

But not his sons, Bogdan and Juliusz. Tragically they had been killed in January that year in a Soviet bombardment of his hometown. Helena was spared because she had gone to send a package to Gajowniczek.

In 1946, the couple moved to Brzeg, near Wrocław. They had no more children but mourned for the ones they had lost.

THE PRIEST

In 1949, the beatification process for Father Kolbe began. On 12 May 1955, Kolbe was recognized by the Holy See as a Servant of God. On 30 January 1969, Kolbe was declared venerable by Pope Paul VI, then beatified as a Confessor of the Faith by the same Pope in 1971. Gajowniczek was a guest at the beatification with Helena.

Finally Kolbe was canonized as a saint by Pope John Paul II on 10 October 1982 and Gajowniczek was again in attendance. Helena had died the same year. Their home became a hub for visitors, including a memorable pilgrimage of religious superiors from Kolbe's monastery in Japan. Gajowniczek travelled many times across Europe and the United States, where, in 1989, he met President George H. W. Bush at the White House.

Gajowniczek died in the city of Brzeg on 13 March 1995 at the age of 93. He was buried at Niepokalanów, the religious community founded by Maximilian Kolbe.

THE REPORT

"On 13 April 1942, some one thousand of us were loaded into closed freight cars at the reception center at Sered. The doors of the cars were sealed..."

So begins what became known as the Vrba–Wetzler report, 33 typewritten pages giving a first-hand account of Auschwitz which would stun the world, and, for the first time, expose that the concentration camp was not just a prisoner-of-war camp – it was a death machine, the likes of which had never been seen. Published on 25 November 1944, the report made clear that the worst nightmares of the Allied governments, and of all of humanity, were being realized in a remote place in Poland. No longer could the world look away.

That the report existed was a miracle in itself. Vrba and Wetzler were only able to report first-hand because they had done something few others achieved, especially after 1942. They had escaped from Auschwitz.

Rudolf Vrba was born in 1924 in Topoľčany, Czechoslovakia. His actual name was Walter Rosenberg – he took the name Rudolf Vrba after his escape.

The Rosenbergs owned a steam sawmill in nearby Jaklovce. When Vrba was 16, Czechoslovakia became a client state of the Nazis and introduced restrictions on Jews' education, housing and travel. Vrba had to leave school and wear a yellow star, as did all the Jews of Czechoslovakia. He continued to study in secret, particularly chemistry. He also met his future wife, Gerta Sidonová.

In February 1942, he decided to leave and join the Czechoslovak Army in exile in England. He set off in a taxi for the border, aged 17, with a map, a box of matches and the equivalent of £10 from his mother. He did not make it. He was arrested on the Hungarian border, and on 15 June 1942 he was taken to the Majdanek concentration camp in Lublin, in German-occupied Poland. He was there for two weeks, briefly meeting his brother, who he never saw again, and encountering for the first time the brutality of his Nazi overseers. Prisoners were beaten for talking to each other or moving too slowly. At roll call each morning, prisoners who had died during the night were piled up behind the living. His head and body were shaved, and he was given a uniform, wooden shoes and a cap. The dehumanization had begun. On 29 June he was sent to Auschwitz.

He later said that he considered trying to escape on the train, but the SS announced that ten men would be shot for every one who went missing.

Sent there at the same time was a man named Alfréd Wetzler. Wetzler was born in Nagyszombat, Austria-Hungary (now Trnava, Slovakia). After his birthplace became part of Czechoslovakia, he was a worker in Trnava from 1936 to 1940. He was arrested in 1942 as a political prisoner and sent to Auschwitz. There he met Rudolf Vrba with whom he would later write the report.

THE REPORT

Vrba was by then a veteran of the camp, but he was still in a state of shock about what he was seeing and what he was suffering. Shortly after arriving he had 44070 tattooed on his wrist. Then he and 400 other men were beaten, and he was "purchased" by a camp commander in exchange for a lemon, such was the value of human life.

He was then assigned to the job of cleaning out the trains that had brought the new arrivals. Most were dead, and the task would take several hours. He told the documentary maker Claude Lanzmann in 1978 that the process relied on speed and making sure no panic broke out. If there was panic the next transport would be delayed and many on the train would die. Thus he felt he was colluding with the Nazis, to help the Jews.

As Vrba put it later, the whole "murder machinery" depended on one principle: that the people coming to Auschwitz didn't know where they were going or for what purpose. Anybody who tried to communicate with newcomers was either clubbed to death or taken behind the wagon and shot.

In 1943, Vrba caught typhus and nearly died – his weight plummeted to 43 kilograms (7 stone). Bedridden, but with a view of the arrivals, he started to keep track of the numbers arriving. From 18 August 1942 to 7 June 1943, he told Lanzmann in 1978, he had seen at least 200 trains arrive, each containing 1,000–5,000 people. He estimated 90 per cent were murdered. In 1961 Vrba swore in an affidavit for the trial of Adolf Eichmann that he believed 2.5 million had been murdered overall in the camp, plus or minus 10 per cent.

He needed people to know.

Vrba began to plan to escape. A Soviet captain with whom he discussed his plans told him he would need Russian tobacco soaked in petrol, then dried, to fool the dogs; a watch to use as a compass; matches to light a fire to cook food; and salt for nutrition. Vrba started to collect these provisions, all the while making notes for his report.

For instance – on 6 March 1944 Vrba heard that the Czech family camp, totalling over 5,000 souls, was about to be sent to the gas chambers. These were women and children who had arrived in September 1943. Normally they would have been gassed immediately, but Adolf Eichmann, high up in the Nazi command, believed that the Red Cross was about to visit the camp, so he kept them alive for propaganda purposes. When the visit failed to materialize, it was decided they would all be killed. On 7 March, 3,791 were gassed, with 11 twins kept alive for medical experiments. None of this was unusual for Auschwitz – what was unusual was that the world would hear of it.

Vrba's desire to escape grew stronger. In early 1944 he learned that the Nazis were preparing for the arrival of Hungary's entire Jewish population of around 1 million people, who were to be exterminated. It was then that he teamed up with Wetzler. For all Vrba's passion, he was not as practical as his compatriot. He later said that Wetzler planned the escape. And he did it very well.

The pair analyzed previous unsuccessful escape attempts and planned a successful one. According to Wetzler, the camp underground helped organize the escape, and supplied information for Vrba and Wetzler to carry. Information

THE REPORT

about the camp, including a sketch of the crematorium, was hidden inside two metal tubes.

On 7 April 1944, during work duties, the pair climbed inside a hollowed-out space they had prepared in a pile of wood stacked between Auschwitz-Birkenau's inner and outer perimeter fences. They surrounded themselves with strong-smelling petrol-soaked Russian tobacco to deter the sniffer dogs.

When they failed to return after their shift, a huge manhunt began, with guards searching everywhere in the area. Still the men stayed in the woodpile. They kept strips of flannel across their mouths to muffle coughing. Wetzler wrote that they lay there counting for "nearly eighty hours. Four thousand eight hundred minutes. Two hundred and eighty-eight thousand seconds."

The plan was to stay there until they got the signal the search had ended – it was given after four days by another prisoner urinating next to the pile. At 9 p.m. on 10 April, they crawled out. Vrba would later describe how weak they were, and how long it took for their circulation to return. The men headed south towards Czechoslovakia 130 kilometres (81 miles) away, walking parallel to the Soła River.

On 13 April, lost in Bielsko-Biala, they approached a farmhouse and a Polish woman took them in for a day. On 16 April they were shot at by German troops but managed to escape. They finally crossed the Polish–Slovak border near Skalité on 21 April 1944. The walk had taken the pair 11 days, without food or water.

They were taken in by a peasant family, and a Jewish doctor, Dr Pollack, was brought in to help them recover.

Pollack's parents and siblings had been taken to Auschwitz, and it was instantly clear to him, based on the escapees' evidence, what their fate would have been.

Soon after, they made contact with the Slovak Jewish Council. They were separated and interviewed about their accounts of Auschwitz independently, so the two testimonies could be compared and verified. A report was then written and rewritten, and translated into German and Hungarian, becoming the 33-page document that would come to be known as the Vrba–Wetzler report, part of the Auschwitz Protocols.

The report contained descriptions of the camp, including detailed descriptions of the gas chambers at Auschwitz and the process of sending prisoners to the gas chambers, until that time just a rumour to the outside world. Much of the report was devoted to Vrba's painstakingly remembered details of the transports that had arrived at Auschwitz – including the nationalities and numbers of those who arrived, an astonishing feat of memory and of secrecy.

Both escapees were struck by the difference between what they had experienced and what the Jewish community had imagined. Wetzler later said how surprised he was by the naïveté of the question, "Is it so difficult to get out of there?" And while there had been rumours of gas chambers, they were not generally believed, or they were believed to be a form of capital punishment – not a mass killing machine.

Vrba grew more and more frustrated as he tried to make the people he was speaking to understand. Finally, he said, the words flowed from him "like a torrent".

THE REPORT

When Wetzler spoke, every word, he later wrote, had "the effect of a blow on the head". He told them about the gas chambers, about the beatings, about the tortures. He also handed over the label from a Zyklon B canister, which he had hidden on himself when he left.

At the end of the testimony, one of the group said that they would type up the report in three days. Vrba exploded in rage. He knew hundreds more died every time there was a hesitation. Something had to be done immediately.

The pair decided to write up the report themselves. They provided details of the horrors that were occurring and drew detailed maps of the camp, which were later found to be incredibly accurate. They also provided, where possible, prisoner names and the assumed number of dead, based on each chamber being able to take 600 inmates daily.

The report was completed by Thursday, 27 April 1944 and was first published in Geneva in May 1944, in German, by the World Jewish Congress. By June 1944 British and American media were reporting the reality of the Auschwitz-Birkenau death camp. World leaders made direct appeals to the Hungarian government to stop the deportation of Jews, which they did on 9 July. They briefly resumed in November when the Nazis overthrew the Hungarian government. The actions of the two men saved tens of thousands of lives – according to some, between 70,000 and 100,000.

It would later be revealed that Allied governments had good intelligence that Jews were being killed en masse from about 1942, but the sheer numbers remained a shock, as did the brutal efficiency with which it was being carried out.

STORIES OF HOPE FROM AUSCHWITZ

After the war Vrba studied chemistry in Prague. He married a childhood friend, Gerta Sidonová, who studied medicine. In 1958 they divorced, but both defected, he to Israel and she to England. He also moved to England, becoming a British citizen in 1966, and then later to Canada.

Wetzler also moved, to Czechoslovakia. He worked as an editor, then as a civil servant, passing away in 1988. He was posthumously awarded the Czech Republic's highest honour, and there is a park named after him in his hometown.

Vrba and Wetzler – two heroes of Auschwitz and bringers of hope.

THE RUSSIAN

Given the hell on earth that Auschwitz was to become for the Jews, and the sheer number who perished there, it can be easy to forget that not all the victims were Jewish – nor all of the survivors.

Before Auschwitz became the Auschwitz we are familiar with, it generally housed political prisoners and prisoners of war, mostly Polish or Soviet. While Hitler and Stalin had signed a non-aggression pact on 24 August 1939, Hitler had broken it on 22 June 1941 by launching a massive attack on the Soviet Union in Operation Barbarossa. Stalin declared war immediately, and the greatest number of deaths suffered by any country in the World War was by Russia, with estimates of between 20 and 27 million Russians losing their lives.

At Auschwitz, credible figures put Russian deaths at around 15,000, most occurring before the installation of the gas chambers. Soviet prisoners began arriving at the camp in July 1941, a mere month after hostilities began. Hitler had already issued guidelines for the treatment of Soviet prisoners in March 1941, before he had even broken the pact. They called for the liquidation of political commissars and communists, especially among soldiers. Communists found in prisoner-of-war camps – which under the Soviet Union meant anyone in the Red Army – were to be taken to the nearest concentration camp and executed. One such group of about 600 Soviet prisoners of war was brought to Auschwitz in the first days of September 1941 and taken to the cellars of Block 11. They were to suffer the first experiment with Zyklon B, and it was to prove effective – there were no survivors.

Another 10,000 arrived in October 1941. On arrival they had to strip naked and immerse themselves in disinfectant, before being released into the camp, still naked. The winter of 1941 was exceptionally cold, and several died immediately. It would be a few days before they received clothing. They also became the first prisoners to be tattooed with a registration number.

In November and December 1941, a special Gestapo commission selected a group of about a thousand prisoners of war (300 "fanatical communists" and 700 "politically undesirable"), who were murdered – some were shot, and the others killed in the gas chamber in the main camp. German soldiers took particular pleasure in torturing their enemy combatants to death, and death rates among the Soviet prisoners were the highest among any group until the gas chambers were fully operational.

As the camp took in more and more Jews, it took in fewer Soviet prisoners, and they were more often kept alive to help carry out hard labour – the Nazi policy of enslaving the fit and healthy and using them to work until they died was now in place.

THE RUSSIAN

It was into this new reality at Auschwitz that Yevgeny Kovalev, a 15-year-old Russian partisan, arrived in 1942. He had been arrested for helping to blow up railways and trains to sabotage the Nazi invaders and stop them heading east into Russia. When he was captured, the Nazis' treatment of him was immediately brutal – he was tied up and whipped, his shirt left soaked in blood.

He was then sent to Auschwitz, where, apart from the horrors of his own situation, he was appalled to see the treatment of the Jewish population. Having been trained in the normal practices of warfare, he was especially shocked that the victims were civilians, which is completely outside the laws of war – something grotesque it is easy to forget when we know the history of the Holocaust so well. The crematoria, he remembered, worked around the clock, with smoke pouring out day and night, making a terrible smell.

At some point, teenagers such as Kovalev were sent to a subcamp that had previously been used for Roma and Sinti prisoners. His barracks were full of the clothing of previous victims, mostly children. Another barracks had packs of human hair stacked up.

He did what he could to help anyone he could. As a worker and a non-Jew, he received slightly higher rations, and he shared what he could, however he could. But the bodies kept piling up.

In late 1944, he was sent to northern Czechoslovakia as forced labour in a radio factory, where he remained working until April 1945, three months after Auschwitz had been liberated. At the end of the war he joined the Soviet military for a time, and then spent the rest of his life working in an automobile plant. He also kept in touch with other survivors – there were 92 Russians listed as being Auschwitz prisoners at liberation – who had also seen the horrors of Auschwitz.

Kovalev shares with many of the survivors a hatred of anti-Semitism. It has been his life's mission to tell of what happened, and to make sure it never happens again. The lesson we can learn from this, he has always said, is that in the end it is hope that wins. Even in the worst of conditions, that light cannot be put out. On the 75th anniversary of the liberation, in 2020, he spoke at the commemoration, sharing his vision of hope.

CONVOY 71

There were, in total, 79 convoys. These trains went from Occupied France into Germany, mostly from Drancy internment camp to Auschwitz. They transported French Jews. Between 27 March 1942 and 17 August 1944, some 73,853 Jews were taken on this journey. We have some approximate numbers of what happened to them. According to the records, 46,802, including children, were gassed on arrival. Of those selected to work, 17,160 were men and 8,703 were women. The total number of survivors when the camp was liberated out of the 73,853 was 2,560 – 1,647 men and 913 women. The other 71,293 were dead.

The effect of the Holocaust on French Jews, and the sheer number who were sent to Auschwitz, has always played a minor role in histories of World War Two. When France fell to the Nazis in 1940, the Final Solution had not been fully thought out and agreed upon, and there was no immediate transfer of anti-Jewish legislation as there had been in other defeated nations. The survival rate of Jews in France was 75 per cent, which is the highest of all nations under Nazi rule – but 25 per cent of the French Jewish population were murdered.

STORIES OF HOPE FROM AUSCHWITZ

On each of those 79 trains there were, no doubt, remarkable men and women, many of whom may never have their stories told. And their stories no doubt contain as much beauty, tragedy and hope as the stories we do encounter. But there is one convoy in particular that stands out in French history and legend for a series of remarkable women who not only went to Auschwitz but survived, and then returned to create astonishing work, both about their experiences and on wider topics. We have already met one of these women, Simone Veil (see page 95), who now lies in the Pantheon, honoured for her contribution to women's rights. But the others were in many ways no less remarkable.

When Convoy 71 set off from Drancy on 13 April 1944, those inside could not have known what awaited them. As with so many who were taken to Auschwitz, they may have heard rumours about the camp, but even those in authority were only just beginning to understand the full horror of these slaughterhouses. The general public, even the Jewish population, knew very little.

Drancy itself gave no sense of its horrifying purpose. Built as a modernist urban community hub in 1940, including the first high-rise residential apartment towers in France, it was confiscated by the Nazi government after the Fall of France. It was used first as police barracks, then converted into the primary detention centre in the Paris region for holding Jews and other people labelled by the Nazis as "undesirable" before they were deported to Germany.

On 20 August 1941, the first raids to collect French Jews occurred in the 11th arrondissement of Paris, on the Right Bank of the Seine. Some 4,000 Jews were taken to Drancy,

CONVOY 71

which was now behind barbed wire. It was the first of many such raids – Drancy was designed to take 700 individuals, but at its peak held more than 7,000 in cramped and unsanitary conditions. On 3 July 1943 the Nazi government took direct control of Drancy from the French. The raids and the deportations increased. Max Jacob, the painter who was Pablo Picasso's closest friend when he first came to Paris, died there, while the artist Charlotte Salomon was there briefly before being sent to Auschwitz on 7 October 1944, when five months pregnant. She was gassed on arrival.

But even at its worst, Drancy was no Auschwitz, so those boarding Convoy 71, as fearful as they may have been, cannot have guessed what lay ahead.

One of them was Ginette Kolinka. Kolinka was born Ginette Cherkasky in Paris in 1925, the youngest of her parents' six daughters. Her parents were non-religious Jews. Her father's family was from Ukraine, while her mother was Romanian. The family lived above her father's manufacturing shop.

She was 15 when France fell to the Nazis. The Cherkaskys decided to head south into what was known as the "free zone" – Ginette, her parents, Léon and Berthe, and her younger brother, 12-year-old Gilbert. Her father managed to obtain forged identity papers, and before they left they made sure that the children had all memorized their new names. In the south, they settled in Avignon.

But on 13 March 1944, Ginette, her father, her brother and a 14-year-old cousin were all arrested by the Gestapo. They had in fact only come for the men, but they arrested

Ginette because she protested. They were put on a train and taken all the way back to Paris and detained at Drancy. Her father was chained to her little brother with handcuffs and her cousin was chained to Szlama Rozenberg, the father of a girl named Marceline.

Marceline, then Rozenberg, but later to be known by her married name Marceline Loridan-Ivens, had been born on 19 March 1928, so she was just coming up to her 16th birthday. At the beginning of the war her family moved to Vaucluse, also in Avignon. Despite her age, she had joined the resistance. She and her father had both been arrested that same morning. They too were taken all the way to Drancy.

When they arrived, Simone Veil was already there, having been arrested on 7 April. Also there, having been arrested on 1 April, was Anne-Lise Stern. Born on 16 July 1921, she was the daughter of Henri Stern, a Freudian psychoanalyst, and Käthe Ruben. Her grandmother had been an active communist in Germany, working with the renowned Rosa Luxemburg. Already 22, Anne-Lise had been a political agitator her whole life. At the start of the war, her family had moved to Nice in the "free zone", where Anne-Lisa had become a close friend of Anna Freud, Sigmund's daughter.

Finally there was Odette Spingarn, born on 14 February 1925 in Le Vésinet, the daughter of antique dealer Henry, and Germaine Créange – both religious Jews. She had one older sister, Alice, who married in 1936 and left Paris. When war broke out in 1940, the family took refuge in the Dordogne, where they lived for three years, before moving to Corrèze. But they were being tracked, and as raids on Jews intensified, they found the noose tightening. On 31 March Odette was arrested. The next day, 1 April, her father was shot. Odette and her mother were taken first to Périgueux, and then on to Drancy.

Convoy 71 set off on 13 April 1944. It was one of the largest of the convoys, with a maximum 1,500 Jews on board. It was also to have the largest complement of people gassed on arrival – 1,265. Only 235 were accepted as workers, including the five women we have just met.

Ginette would later describe the shock of the arrival – as ever, the new arrivals were stripped, shaved and tattooed. At 19, she had never seen another naked female, nor been seen by one. By now a lack of staff at the camp meant that it was fellow inmates who applied the tattoos. She was given her new clothes, an old sweater and a skirt; no underwear. They were sent to the shower, but there was barely any water.

In its desperate state, Auschwitz – both its guards and its inmates – had turned increasingly violent. Later Ginette would say she was "beaten the whole time, all through the day, for nothing, nothing, nothing".

Ginette had also been separated from the male members of her family and would soon find out that her father, Léon, aged 61, and her brother Gilbert, aged 12, were among those immediately sent to be murdered. The fate of her 14-year-old cousin remains a mystery, but we can assume he suffered the same fate.

Anna-Lise was similarly shocked and terrified. She had seen on the train what were known as the Children of Izieu, 44 Jewish children of different nationalities, who took refuge in a house converted into a holiday camp during World War Two in the French commune of Izieu and had been rounded up on the order of the notorious Nazi German officer Klaus Barbie, already well known for torturing prisoners. As soon as the train pulled into Auschwitz, the screaming children were taken to the gas chamber.

For Marceline the greatest shock was to see her father immediately sent to the gas chamber. She would write a book in the form of a letter to him in 2016, some 70 years later, called *But You Did Not Come Back* – a reference to a promise he made her as they were separated. Odette lost her mother, Germaine. At 55 she had been fortunate not to go straight to the gas chamber but unfortunate as she quickly became ill and died on 24 May 1944. By then Odette was working in the Kanada warehouse, helping to itemize articles taken from the inmates.

In the autumn of 1944, as Auschwitz started to crumble, the women were sent on to other places. Odette was sent to work in an Audi factory in Zschopau in Saxony, while the others were all transferred to Bergen-Belsen. Ginette worked in a factory producing aircraft components.

But again they needed to be moved as the Allied armies approached. There was a roll call, and Marceline was found to be missing – she had hidden herself to try and avoid the journey. She was unsuccessful, but in the general atmosphere of despair and chaos, an act that would usually have cost her her life was ignored.

Ginette, meanwhile, was suffering the effects of typhus and becoming increasingly ill, not helped by the stop-start nature of the journey, again a product of no one quite knowing what was going on. It took seven days for the train to reach its destination, Theresienstadt, and many died on the train. When they arrived, Ginette, now critically ill and weighing only 26 kilograms (4 stone), simply threw herself on the ground. Other women from the train had worked out how to drain the water from a locomotive along the track, and they all drank.

Their arrival had in fact coincided with the camp's liberation by the Soviet army. They were startled to find no German soldiers. Medical care was given to all of the surviving women, and their repatriation to France began.

The only woman missing was Odette, who had been working in the Audi factory in Zschopau. On 14 April, all 800 women working there were put on a train which they believed was taking them away to be killed. Odette and 13 other women jumped off the train as it was travelling at full speed – she would later write a memoir called *My Leap to Freedom*. She had three comrades with her, two French and one German. The German woman was Elly (Élisabeth) Fullmann, and after the war, Odette made sure that she received Israel's Medal of the Righteous.

What these women did during their time at Auschwitz and elsewhere already makes them truly remarkable, but their lives after going through such trauma shows the power of hope, resilience and dedication in even the worst circumstances.

Odette Spingarn became a social worker and worked at the children's relief organization Oeuvre de secours aux enfants (OSE). She also provided, at Audi's request, evidence of the company's collaboration with Nazi Germany, with a view to compensation and corporate responsibility-taking. Odette married and had two children. She passed away on 25 March 2020. As requested, her gravestone read "Deported to Auschwitz-Birkenau, registration number 78769".

Ginette married Albert Kolinka on 13 April 1951 and they became market traders. For a long time she could not speak about what she had been through. But then, on the death of her husband in 1993, and with what she perceived as the rise of political parties that flirted with or even embraced racist ideologies, she became a passionate spokesperson on issues of the Holocaust, fighting to ensure it never happens again.

Her lifelong friend, Marceline Rozenberg, became a filmmaker and writer. In 1963, she met and married the documentary director Joris Ivens. She assisted him in his work and co-directed some of his films, including *17th Parallel: Vietnam in War* (1968). They spent time in China during the Cultural Revolution, making a series of 12 films called *How Yukong Moved the Mountains*. In 1993 she wrote and directed the scenario for *La Petite Prairie aux Bouleaux* (*The Birch-Tree Meadow*), her first (and only) feature-length fiction film and the first film ever shot at Birkenau.

Anne-Lise Stern returned from the camps to find that her parents had somehow survived, although most of the rest of her family had not. Aged 24, she wrote a series of essays on her time in the camps, collected into the volume *Textes du retour* (*Essays on Coming Home*), considered by many to be a masterpiece of Holocaust memoir. She then trained as a psychoanalyst, with a focus on hospitalized chronically psychotic children. She was a particular admirer of the famous psychoanalyst Jacques Lacan, whom she credited with having re-established psychoanalysis after Auschwitz. She also held public seminars to fight the rise of Holocaust denial. She died on 6 May 2013.

And we know that Simone Veil was transferred to the Pantheon on 30 June 2018. Marceline Rozenberg – whom Veil always credited with an ability to make other women at the camp laugh – attended at the age of 90, and said that to her, every woman at Auschwitz was also there cheering her on.

Five remarkable women, and five inspiring messages of hope.

A TYPE OF FREEDOM

Most of her good work was done at Terezín, but when she died at Auschwitz everyone knew who she was and what she had done.

Friedl Dicker-Brandeis was an artist and had been a member of the Weimar Bauhaus, the influential group that revolutionized art and design in the early twentieth century. So talented was she that she was awarded scholarships for her studies – an incredibly rare privilege.

She was born in Vienna on 30 July 1898 into a poor Jewish family. Her father was a shop assistant and her mother died when she was only four years old. Some believe that losing her mother helped motivate her to become a substitute mother to many children in the camp.

At 17 she started studying photography and textiles, and took part in street puppet theatre, and then received her scholarship to study drawing under Professor Franz Cižek, who shared her interest in children's art. Her next teacher was Johannes Itten, and she also studied music with the famous Austrian composer Arnold Schoenberg.

But it was when she joined the Bauhaus that her talents flourished, with the director, Walter Gropius, saying of her that he admired "the multifaceted nature of her gifts and her unbelievable energy" and that "already in her first year she began to teach the beginners".

In 1923, she helped establish the Workshops of Fine Art in Berlin, whose products included book covers, textile works and children's toys, as well as stage and costume designs. Soon after she began designing beautiful and functional furniture for children.

In 1931 she started teaching, but in Vienna in 1934 she was briefly arrested for communist activities. Released, she moved to Prague in Czechoslovakia and married an accountant, Pavel Brandeis. She continued to make her own art and to teach children. She also continued with her political activities. New anti-Jewish laws meant she couldn't exhibit her work, but friends organized an exhibition of her art in London in 1940.

In late autumn 1942, she and her husband received a deportation order, were taken into custody and on 17 December 1942 they were sent to Theresienstadt – a concentration camp in Terezín, now in the Czech Republic.

Theresienstadt was a camp with two faces. To the outside world it seemed a model camp, with a rich cultural life – many painters and musicians were sent there, and some of its administration was in Jewish hands. Inmates were free from the usual rules of Nazi censorship and the ban on "degenerate art" – art that did not meet the Nazi standards on realism. There was an orchestra, and a great deal of visual art was produced. It was often used as a propaganda tool, with any filming of concentration camps for outside consumption being carried out there.

A TYPE OF FREEDOM

But it was also a concentration camp, with overcrowded collective dormitories of 60 to 80 people per room. Food was as sparse as elsewhere and, in general, inmates had to work at hard labour for around 70 hours a week. The death rate was lower than at numerous other camps but still very high.

It was also a holding camp – a great many of the inmates who spent time there would later be taken to Auschwitz and gassed.

Friedl immediately started running art classes for the children at Theresienstadt. She also designed sets and costumes for at least two children's performances and made an exhibition of children's drawings. She was, she said, trying to give them their inner lives back.

In 1943 she gave a lecture to the camp entitled "Children's Drawing". Even in the camp, she said, making art gave the children freedom. It gave them hope. She also passed on her message about how to teach children and allow them to be themselves. She believed that childhood was not a preliminary, immature stage on the way to adulthood, and that their creativity should not be stifled but encouraged.

One girl who was taught by her was Erna Furman, who survived the camps and went on to be a psychoanalyst and teacher. She would later write that Friedl's teaching, and the times spent drawing with her, were among the fondest memories of her life. Erna said that Friedl taught without asking anything for herself, which was the ultimate gift.

This giving of herself – the most precious gift of all – would go on to produce some 4,500 children's paintings, which Friedl kept, and many of which are now displayed at

Prague museum. To look at them is heartbreaking – most depict scenes from the camp, the only world many of the children ever knew. Or ever would know, apart from the place to which they would later be taken and where they would be gassed – Auschwitz.

It was a journey that Friedl also ended up taking. In September 1944, her husband was transported to Auschwitz. She volunteered for the next transport to join him. Before she left, she gave Raja Engländerova, chief tutor of Girls' Home L 410, two suitcases containing the 4,500 drawings. As Friedl insisted that each child sign their work, these drawings are some of the only records of existence for many of the children.

There was no time to start anything in Auschwitz – she went straight to the gas chamber, although her husband was spared. But her reputation went before her, and her work remains a testament to hope.

THE SON

"It was a very difficult situation, because I knew that for him it was one of the most important events in his life." – Rolf Mengele

When in 1977 Rolf Mengele heard that his father, the Nazi doctor Josef Mengele from Auschwitz, notorious for his gruesome experiments, and known as the "Angel of Death", had suffered a stroke and wanted to see him in his hideaway in Brazil, he struggled with the idea. Should he go to see this man, his father, whose actions were well known, and who was regarded as one of the twentieth century's most evil men?

It is a problem that has beset many of the children of the butchers of the Holocaust – to have a parent who has carried out unspeakable crimes is to carry a sentence for life. Brigitte Höss, daughter of Rudolf Höss, commandant of Auschwitz, suffered so much distress that after the war she left Germany and moved to the US, to live in anonymity. "He was very good to me," she has said of him. He read her fairy tales, taught her to ride horses. Meanwhile he was gassing hundreds of Jews a day.

Hermann Göring, the second most powerful Nazi after Hitler, always made sure he was home to kiss his daughter Edda goodnight, while Heinrich Himmler, chief architect of the Final Solution, was a doting father, regularly sending his daughter chocolates when he was away and calling her several times a day, before going back to work to plan the extermination of the Jews.

At the end of the war, Josef Mengele had fled, hiding on a farm in Germany. Through his SS contacts he managed to get away to Genoa and then Argentina. His wife refused to go with him, and they divorced by proxy soon after.

He returned to Germany just once, in 1956, under an alias. He met with his son Rolf, then 12, in Zurich. Rolf was told Mengele was his "Uncle Fritz". This was their only contact, until Rolf went to see him in Brazil.

Rolf decided that the only thing he could do was to confront his father with his crimes. As he admitted, he danced around the subject for two days, but then could hold on no longer – how could his father do this?

According to Rolf, "he exploded" and asked how it was possible that his son could believe he was capable of those things. He claimed the accusations were all lies, were all propaganda. But Rolf knew the truth of what were not allegations but facts produced by hundreds of witnesses. His father was, he said later, an "unrepentant Nazi". When he left he felt nothing but disturbed by this man. "I would have preferred another father," was his understated quote in a 1985 documentary.

Josef Mengele died soon after seeing his son. On 7

THE SON

February 1979, he had a second stroke while swimming and drowned.

Can hope be found here? Perhaps. Rolf passed on the documents bequeathed to him by his father about his life in South America after the war, which enabled Nazi hunters to trace a number of former National Socialists and their networks. In most cases, the children of those who perpetrated the Holocaust have tried, where possible, to find ways to repay at least some of the debt. It is yet another way that the victims of Auschwitz have defeated those who tried to destroy them.

BY CHANCE ALONE

It is a question anyone who survived the camps is confronted with – why did they survive when so many others didn't? Survivor's guilt is a well-known phenomenon, and while it is in no way exclusive to the Holocaust, a great many survivors have fallen victim to it. In fact, the term was first proposed in exploring the mental health of concentration camp survivors, and it was a survivor of Auschwitz who proposed it – the Dutch psychiatrist, Eddy de Wind.

De Wind had noticed in his patients, when he returned to the Netherlands after the war, a cluster of symptoms which seemed to afflict them all. As well as anxiety and depression, sleep disturbance and nightmares, mood swings and struggling in social situations, there was an associated feeling of guilt, which seemed to grow greater as time passed, meaning it was both a chronic and a progressive disease.

He termed this "concentration camp syndrome" (or KZ syndrome on account of the German term *Konzentrationslager*). This was one of the first diagnoses of what we would now call post-traumatic stress disorder (PTSD).

De Wind shared many of these symptoms, and it was the guilt that interested him most – all of those who had survived had done so, ultimately, due to good luck and/or random chance.

For those who had lost family members, the guilt seemed particularly acute. A parent who survived while their child died, or a child who survived while a parent died – and all the other possible combinations across families.

This feeling of guilt has led to a high number of suicides among survivors – in death they become the same as those they mourn. But it has also led to some positive outcomes. One thing that has united a large number of Auschwitz survivors, including the majority of those featured in this book, has been the idea of "bearing witness". It is not enough just to survive, it is their duty to tell others what happened, either to ensure justice for the victims or to be a part of the battle to never let this happen again.

Eddy de Wind's own story is a remarkable one.

Born in 1916, he studied medicine and was the last Jewish student to graduate from Leiden University before Jews were banned from studying. Soon after, he was taken into custody on 23 February 1941, during a mass arrest of Jews in Amsterdam's Old Jewish Quarter – 427 on that one day. The men were all beaten and then underwent medical examinations. Of those 427 arrests, later records show that only three men survived the Holocaust.

De Wind got away by, with 11 others, pretending he had tuberculosis. Released, they zigzagged away from the station for fear of being shot in the back as they left.

But de Wind felt – even then – guilt. His mother had been arrested and sent to the Dutch transit/concentration camp Westerbork – and he immediately volunteered to go there as well on the proviso he could be used as a doctor. This was agreed to, and he was sent the next day.

But when de Wind got to Westerbork, he learned his mother had already been sent to Auschwitz and was undoubtedly dead. Now a prisoner, he started work as the camp doctor as promised, though this mostly involved the gruesome task of selecting who remained fit for work and who should be sent on the next transport. He would have declared them all fit, but there were quotas to be met.

Then a moment of hope and of light. In that most inhuman place, he fell in love – that most human of emotions – with one of the nurses working in the same barracks as him, Friedel Komornik. They got engaged and were married in March 1943. There is a photograph of the couple on their wedding day, surrounded by friends and with a large bouquet of flowers – it is hard to reconcile this with the fact they were still in the camp.

Later in 1943, they were both sent to Auschwitz too – not to be gassed, but for their medical skills. De Wind worked in the medical barracks, which meant contact with Josef Mengele, who asked about infectious diseases at Westerbork and in the Netherlands. His wife was condemned to Block 10, to "provide care" during Mengele's experiments on women.

Unable to see each other but still flushed with love, the pair found ways to exchange notes. Keeping secrets at

Auschwitz was always to risk one's life, and it was a risk they were prepared to take.

As Auschwitz started to wind down its operations, de Wind was devastated to see his wife heading off on one of the notorious death marches, with him left behind. They were, remarkably, reunited when they both got back to the Netherlands.

But something had changed, in him, in her, in them, as it did in all those who were dealing with their return. De Wind and Friedel separated, a not uncommon occurrence among survivors.

What he did not know is that, in fact, KZ syndrome would, for reasons that are not absolutely clear, tend to be at its worst about 30 years after the trauma, and the trauma often seems to be passed on to the children of survivors.

And finally, as de Wind's son told *The Times of Israel*, there was what would come to be known as "victim envy". Those who returned home often had to deal with complex personal and social arrangements, with partners, families and friends who could not understand. They had to deal with finances, sometimes with getting homes, sometimes with getting jobs. They had to deal with getting their health back or knowing that they couldn't.

Those who had died had to deal with none of that. Might one feel some envy for how simple things were for them? But could one, and keep an easy conscience? This is a classic trauma: two irreconcilable ideas.

One thing that de Wild had to deal with was publishing a memoir – astonishingly he had managed to write it while in the camps, possibly making it the only "real time" account of being an inmate in Auschwitz. His decision to publish straight after the war was due to a promise he had made to a young Dutch woman named Roosje he met as they were leaving Auschwitz, who was afraid no one would believe the stories they had to tell when they returned home.

The book did not sell well initially. His son believes that this was because of the desire of everyone to try and turn away, just as Roosje had feared. But later *Last Stop Auschwitz* became one of the most important books about the most dreadful of the camps.

It may be drawing a long bow to see hope in the story of yet more layers of trauma caused by this camp – and yet not every lesson learned from the Holocaust is a simple one. Eddy de Wind opened up a way of looking at trauma that has not only helped sufferers of KZ syndrome but made us all aware that human reactions are complicated things, and that there are ways to intervene and to care.

THE AUSCHWITZ UPRISING

He was not Roma or Sinti himself, but the Polish political prisoner Tadeusz Joachimowski will always be a hero to those communities for two acts of extraordinary courage and cunning, which not only saved lives but allowed the history of Roma and Sinti victims of Auschwitz to be remembered and written about.

Most people are familiar with the Final Solution to the Jewish Problem, which was one of the fundamental aims of the Third Reich, and of the construction of the death camps like Auschwitz. But many are less familiar with the Final Solution to the Gypsy Problem – "gypsy" (*Zigeuner*) being the designation given to Roma and Sinti people.

The original plan had been simply to deport all Roma and Sinti from what had become known as Greater Germany, and between 1940 and 1941, a large number were sent away. But as the attempted extermination of the Jews began in earnest, it was decided that a similar process would be the most effective for other groups the Nazis believed to be "racially inferior". Some Roma and Sinti were in fact moved into Jewish ghettos, such as the one at Łódź, but in December 1942, SS Chief Heinrich Himmler ordered that most Sinti and Roma people in Nazi Germany were to be deported to Auschwitz-Birkenau. A special camp – called the Gypsy Family Camp – was set up there in the spring of 1943, and Roma and Sinti deported from many other occupied countries ended up there. Around 23,000 would pass through it, a quarter of them children under 14.

Remarkably, some of them were members of the German army. Among them were many who had been decorated for bravery and valour in World Wars One and Two. They were especially proud of these medals and believed that because of them they would be treated in a better way. They believed that they had been arrested by mistake. They were shocked to find that wasn't the case.

At Auschwitz there were 38 barracks for Roma and Sinti prisoners, lining two sides of a street. Prisoners were housed in 32 of these. There were also separate buildings in the camp with washrooms, toilets and what was called the "sauna". This was a room where prisoners were brought upon arriving at the camp and forced to strip, undergo disinfection, be tattooed and registered.

Unusually, men, women and children all lived together. While some might see this as an advantage, this crowding in confined space, according to Roma historians, caused the violation of all cultural rules regulating the relations between Roma of different genders, ages and group affiliations. There was also sexual violence against women by guards.

For all that, according to one witness, the inmates worked hard to stick together. There was a sense of solidarity, with individuals offering each other help; there were no fights or quarrels, and families disciplined their little children. Family ties were, he said, very strong. In the barracks they tried – despite the inhuman hygienic conditions – to keep order and cleanness.

Other aspects of Auschwitz life remained sickeningly familiar – the inmates' clothes were replaced with striped prison garb, heads were shaved, and they received their tattoo, with a Z in front of it to designate "*Zigeuner*". They were also made to wear a black triangle on their clothing, the symbol of the prisoner group termed "asocial" by the Nazis.

And, of course, Dr Mengele was carrying out his activities – with so many children as part of the camp, he ordered a daycare facility be built, where the children would be left by their parents when they went off to their forced labour. Mengele performed his experiments on these children in particular.

The conditions, as with so much of the camp, were terrible, exacerbated by the group being regarded as the last in line when it came to the already scarce food and medical help. It is estimated that around half of the Roma and Sinti inmates died from starvation, overcrowding and the unsanitary conditions. The catastrophic hygienic conditions in the barracks soon led to the spread of infectious diseases, including typhoid.

Others died from hard labour and if there was no "real" work to be done, as with other inmates, Roma and Sinti were given pointless back-breaking tasks: digging up turf or clay and then replacing it, shifting piles of sand and stones from one place to another, before returning it the next day. Prisoners who could not keep up with the set pace were beaten, which, in combination with their physical exhaustion, sometimes led to their death.

After they returned from work, the evening roll calls followed, which could take hours, especially when one of the prisoners was missing or had tried to escape. In this case, the roll call lasted until the SS guards managed to catch the prisoner and brought him back to the camp.

And then there were those taken to the gas chambers. In late March 1943, the SS murdered approximately 1,700 Roma from the Białystok region in the gas chambers – they had only arrived a few days earlier. These were not even registered as having been at the camp.

That same month, a Polish political prisoner named Tadeusz Joachimowski was transferred to the Roma section and tasked with registering all the Sinti and Roma people there, from the spring of 1943 until the summer of 1944.

Joachimowski was born on 25 June 1908 in Żnin, Poland. Having been arrested for anti-Nazi activities in 1940, he was imprisoned in Tarnów Prison in southern Poland, before being transferred to Auschwitz in 1942, and then to the "Gypsy Camp".

It was in May 1944 that he made his first courageous intervention into affairs in the camp, as he described when he gave testimony in 1960 to the Polish historian Danuta Czech.

On 15 May 1944, Camp Commander (Georg) Bonigut told him things looked bad for the Gypsy Camp – the decision had been made to demolish it. Everyone who was still living there – the population was around 6,500 – was to be gassed. Bonigut told Joachimowski to inform the

THE AUSCHWITZ UPRISING

inmates and tell them to stay in their barracks when the SS came.

They came the next day, about 50 of them, and tried to enter the barracks. They were met with complete silence. According to Joachimowski, the inmates had managed to man themselves armed with knives, shovels, iron, crowbars and stones. They did not leave the barracks. There was a tense stand-off, and then the SS men, without clear orders, left. They did not return.

While the entire population of the camp would later be killed, news of the uprising spread through Auschwitz, and for many was the first indication that the implacable air of strength of the SS was starting to crumble as the war turned, and a sense that Nazi Germany was going to pay a price for its crimes set in. It is also viewed with pride by Roma and Sinti communities confronted with the awful facts of the concentration camp.

At the end of July, Joachimowski made another intervention. It had been decided that the Gypsy Camp would now be demolished and everything inside it would be destroyed, and the inmates reassigned. Joachimowski realized this would include all of the records he had meticulously kept: names, surnames, birthdates, professions, and where the Roma or Sinti prisoners were from.

To lose these records would be to lose these people completely. It has been speculated that one of the things that made the collection and murder of the Jews possible was that they were often easily traceable, having a long history of keeping detailed administrative records. With the Roma and Sinti, it was different – their lifestyle, often nomadic, meant there were few written records, and much that was known within the community was by oral transmission. More than with most communities, to kill a Roma or Sinti, then, was not just to kill an individual but a storehouse of knowledge.

So Joachimowski decided to act. During the night, he broke into the now deserted camp and stole the two main lists of prisoners he had worked on, assisted by two other Polish prisoners, Ireneusz Pietrzyk and Henryk Porębski. He then wrapped them up in pieces of men's clothing and stored them in a zinc bucket with a wooden cover, before burying them in the grounds of the camp.

On 13 January 1949 the three men managed to secure permission to return to the camp and dug the lists up. The books were quite wet, so their first few pages had been damaged and were illegible. Otherwise they were in good condition and became the main source of information on the Roma and Sinti imprisoned at Auschwitz-Birkenau. Thousands of victims of Auschwitz were listed, helping families to identify loved ones, and prosecutors to build evidence against the camp commanders and SS guards. Without these records, everyone listed would have disappeared from history. It seems a small act, but had any of the three men been caught, they would have been killed.

It was shortly after the camp was taken apart that the near total extermination of the Roma and Sinti took place. On 2 August 1944, a long cargo train was moved to the railway ramp. The Roma and Sinti who had been designated for transport to the Ravensbrück and Buchenwald concentration

THE AUSCHWITZ UPRISING

camps were assembled by the train. They then said goodbye through the fence to those remaining in the camp.

As soon as the train left, at about 7 p.m., members of the Sonderkommando (prisoners, usually Jews, who were forced to help with the disposal of gas chamber victims) entered the housing blocs and drove all the remaining prisoners out. On their way, they had to pass Joachimowski, sitting at his table, counting them as they passed. There were 4,200 of them.

They understood they would be taken away to the gas chambers, where they would be gassed. Most of them were children, elders and women. Witnesses said they left their barracks shouting, weeping and wailing. All were killed.

The only members of the community not sent to the gas chambers were twin children. As Joachimowski watched on, Josef Mengele drove them back into the barracks. He heard regular gun shots. Mengele was shooting them, and he would go on to perform autopsies as part of his "research".

The tragic events of the Nazi genocide of Roma and Sinti are gradually becoming better acknowledged in world history. In 1965 compensation started to be paid by the West German government to the families of victims, as identified from Joachimowski's list, and in March 1982 Federal Chancellor Helmut Schmidt formally stated that German Roma had been victims of genocide.

Each year on 2 August, remembrance services are held, bringing together representatives of Roma organizations and governments, diplomats, survivors and witnesses not only from Europe but the rest of the world. In 2023, the wife of survivor Horst Pohl, Gerda Pohl spoke at this event of the long-lasting effects of the war on her husband, and his fear of medical treatment having been part of Mengele's experiments – he died at 54, which Gerda put down to the trauma of the camps. She finished with a note of hope and defiance, asking that everyone fight racism wherever they encounter it, especially young people who had the future of Germany and Europe in their hands.

Since 2002, Roma victims of Nazism have also been included in the agenda of the International Holocaust Day of 27 January, which commemorates the liberation of the Auschwitz concentration camp in 1945.

As part of the permanent exhibition, all known Roma and Sinti victims of Auschwitz are listed – a fact made possible by the actions of Tadeusz Joachimowski, a man who would not let go of his humanity, or his hope.

THE COMMOTION

As Rachel Levy remembers it, by the time she got to Auschwitz, there was very little happening. It was no longer strict, she and those around her just vegetated in the barracks and talked about food.

She was born Ruzena Levy, in Bhutz in Czechoslovakia in 1930. She, her father, mother, older brother and three younger siblings lived a happy rural life, as part of a small village. Then, in 1942, the Nazis came to the village and took away all the young men, including her father. She never heard from him again. She later found out that he had died in the forced labour camps.

When the authorities came back, the family's neighbours tried to protect them, hiding them for a while, but they were threatened that they would be killed if they helped Jews, so they gave up. The family was moved briefly to a ghetto and then taken to the train. Old people, young people, sick people – they all had to stand the whole time. It was, she later said, hell.

She clung onto her mother, who in turn clung onto her other children, including her baby brother, not yet three. Her other brother was two years older than her, and he was silent all the way. He would remain that way for most of the rest of his life. They didn't know where they were going – and where they were going was Auschwitz.

On arrival, there was immediate selection. Levy and her brother were put in the line to survive, her mother and younger siblings were put in the other queue. As new arrivals, they did not know that the other queue was for the gas chambers, but they were soon told.

Her mother, she remembered, pushed her towards the other line and kept saying, *"shtark, shtark"*, which means "strong" in Yiddish. That was the last time Levy saw her and her two little sisters and her baby brother. She would later find out that her grandparents, aunts, uncles and great-grandfather were also all killed in the Holocaust.

By the time Rachel arrived at Auschwitz, the camp was beginning to come to pieces, which is why there was little work to do. But conditions remained horrific and unhygienic. And if anything, the treatment by the guards only became more brutal as a sense ran through the camp that they were going to be defeated.

But nothing was certain, and one day the doors of the block were flung open, and Dr Josef Mengele strode in. Rachel, her friend Zelde and a group of other girls were ordered out of the block and sent towards the gates of the gas chambers.

It was then that one of the small miracles happened that can change fate forever and bring hope. As they stood there waiting near the kitchens, people came out carrying soup in great big urns, and somebody made a commotion. She didn't know who started it, but as it continued, people started moving around, and there were gunshots.

THE COMMOTION

Rachel would never know what the commotion was about – it could have been something as simple as someone bumping into a person carrying soup and spilling it. But her friend Zelde acted quickly. She grabbed Rachel's hand and pulled her away. They hung onto the people from the kitchens and scurried back to the block and safety.

It was her final brush with death at the camp, although she still had to endure the awful conditions, and then a death march to Bergen-Belsen, before that camp was liberated in April 1945.

At first, she and her brother were taken to Belfast, Northern Ireland, and then on to a small village named Millisle, County Down, where a farm was taking in Holocaust survivors. It was freedom, she later said. "It was green and beautiful. We ran towards the sea. We actually tried to go in the water which was icy."

The farm had been taking in refugees since 1939. One that Rachel heard about was one of the early Kindertransport children, Walter Kammerling. Born in 1923 in Vienna, he was 14 when Nazi Germany occupied Austria in March 1938. Walter's parents decided to send him to Britain on the Kindertransport. The age limit for the Kindertransport was 16: Walter was 15 but his sisters, being 17 and 18, could not join him. His eldest sister did manage to get a work visa and also came to Britain. After the war, they would find that their father was sent to Auschwitz-Birkenau on 29 September 1944 and their mother and sister on 23 October 1944. All three were murdered.

After a brief time in a camp for refugee children at Dovercourt in Essex, Walter was moved to the Millisle farm in February 1939, and worked there for three years. Briefly he was threatened with internment as an "enemy alien", but farm work was a "reserved occupation" – that is, it was essential for the war effort, and he was spared.

In 1944 he joined the British Army to continue the fight against Nazi Germany and served in Belgium and the Netherlands. He married a woman who had also been a Kindertransport child, Herta, whose parents and baby brother had also managed to escape to Britain.

After the war, they returned to Vienna for nine years, and had two sons, before moving back to the UK in 1956 – to Bournemouth where Herta's parents had settled. Walter worked as a chartered engineer, was chairman of his synagogue and enjoyed singing, both operatic and Klezmer.

He also went back to education – as with many survivors, he felt he had been cheated out of his schooling when young – and he achieved a degree in maths and music with the Open University.

Rachel Levy moved to London and trained as a dressmaker; she married Phineas, and they had two children. For more than 50 years she could not bring herself to speak about her experiences.

But then in her 70s she began to speak to school and community group about her experiences, as part of her bearing witness, and was awarded a British Empire Medal (BEM). In 2017 she moved into Jewish Care's Selig Court Retirement Living apartments in Golders Green and was presented with a bust of herself which now proudly adorns the apartment.

THE COMMOTION

As any survivor will tell you, fate is a strange thing – had there not been a commotion around a soup urn, Rachel Levy BEM would not have been able to tell her tale, and her children and grandchildren would not exist.

THE TWINS

Dr Josef Mengele's fascination with twins, and the medical experiments he carried out on them, have been well documented. Before Auschwitz, Josef Mengele was an assistant to a well-known researcher who studied twins at the Institute for Hereditary Biology and Racial Hygiene in Frankfurt, and when he moved to the camp in 1943 he found a fertile ground for his studies.

There was also what might be called a "practical" reason for Mengele's interest. In good scientific practice, if you are carrying out an experiment on one thing, it is usual to keep another of the same thing that you don't carry out an experiment on, known as the control or control group. If you want to see the effect of pouring water on a seed you have planted, you plant two and pour water on one. The difference between what happens to them is the effect of pouring the water.

In carrying out experiments on humans, this can be problematic. In social experiments it can be effective, and in some drug trials, but there are ethical considerations – one cannot test the effect of giving food to someone by not giving food to someone else, for example. The experiments are also hampered by the starting difference between two distinct individuals. One may track a smoker and a non-smoker to see which one will die first, but if the non-smoker has genetic markers that can't be identified and that mean they will only live a short time, the connection between smoking and death cannot be definitively established. All that can be done is to carry out as many such experiments as possible to establish a strong causal link.

With twins, Mengele believed he had solved the problem of difference – twins were believed to be absolutely identical in genetic makeup (as we would call it now), so if you made one twin smoke, and the other not, you could find out precisely and definitively the effect of smoking on mortality.

As for the problem of ethics – well, it seems Mengele didn't have any ethics. The experiments he carried out were to be some of the most horrifying in human history.

After he arrived at Auschwitz, Mengele was always there at the selection process, looking for possible subjects. It became part of the greeting that inmates going onto the trains to help remove new arrivals would whisper to the children – they told them to say they were older than they were, and to say, "No twins, no twins". They even forcibly separated obvious twins from each other before they left the train. This might have been condemning them to the gas chambers, but it was saving them from Mengele. In fact, after the war, a few surviving twins would refer to him ironically as the Angel of Auschwitz, a twist on his nickname of the Angel of Death, because they owed their lives to him.

Vera Kriegel and her twin sister Olga were just five years old when they were taken from their village in

THE TWINS

Czechoslovakia to Auschwitz. Vera remembered getting off the train and "treading on the dead bodies like steps". They and their mother were taken to one side and presented to Mengele. He was fascinated, he told them, by the fact that their mother's eyes were blue and she had "perfect Aryan features" – the Nazi dream – but that both girls had brown eyes. Mengele saw this as a regression – why had it occurred? The girls were selected for experimentation. Vera was taken to his laboratory. There she was shocked to find herself looking at a whole wall of human eyes, staring at her "like a collection of butterflies". She fell down on the floor.

Vera would later remember how she was kept naked in a cage, given painful injections directly into her spine, and beaten if she cried, which she did as she saw many other children suffer and die. In another experiment, she says, the pair of them and more than 100 other twins were given injections of bacteria that cause noma disease, resulting in boils and disfigurement.

It was also well known that Mengele would remove organs from one twin without anaesthetic to see how long the child would survive. When they died, the other twin, no longer needed, was murdered. Vera says that he killed people with an injection to the heart, and then he dissected them.

Somehow she and her sister survived. On 26 January 1945, she told the BBC in 2015, the guards were in a big panic. They poured petrol over the barracks and tried to destroy the evidence of what had gone on there. Grabbing a big pack of family photos they had somehow smuggled into the camp, Vera, her mother and sister fled the camp.

But they were caught and locked back in the barracks. They expected to be killed at any moment.

The moment never came. Hours later, all the Germans had left, and the next day the Red Army arrived and the children were filmed for newsreels shown all around the world.

Menachem Bodner was even younger than the Kriegel twins when he arrived at Auschwitz, being a mere three years old. He survived but had no firm memories of his time in the camp except a few scattered images – staring out at barbed wire, running down concrete stairs, hiding in a corner. There was also one vivid memory that he dreamed about every night: the bloodied face of an elderly man.

So young was Menachem that when the camp was liberated he did not even know who he was – only his prisoner number, A-7734. "Menachem Bodner" was the name given to him by the family, also Holocaust survivors, that adopted him. In fact, he had no idea he had a twin. His only "evidence" was another dream he kept having – another boy who looked like him, the same eyes, the same blond hair, sleeping in bed beside him. But a dream is not a lot to go on.

Then 70 years after Auschwitz, he took a DNA test. This was run against the database of Auschwitz survivors. Menachem Bodner was in fact Elias Gottesman, and he had had a twin brother, Jeno – prisoner number A-7735. The two were born in the Mukacheve area in the Carpathian Mountains in Hungary (now Ukraine) and had been taken to the camp in 1944.

Using this information, genealogist Ayana KimRon scoured the records for more information. She found that

THE TWINS

Menachem had cousins in the US, whom he later contacted, and was able to find pictures of his parents, of whom he had no memory. It turned out that his mother, Roza, had survived the camps and managed to return after the war to her hometown, only to be murdered in 1946 by anti-Semitic rioters. His father, Ignatz, had died in the camps.

Both Elias and Jeno Gottesman survived Auschwitz and were taken into care. Elias was adopted and became Menachem, his new parents taking him to Israel, but no record can be found of what happened to Jeno. Social media searches for prisoner A-7735 have not solved the mystery, but the search goes on.

And then there is the remarkable story of two twins who were not each other's twin but became in a deep sense brothers.

Leopold and Miriam Lowy were twins born in Berehove (Beregszasz), in what was then Hungary and is today Ukraine. When they were sent to Auschwitz, they were taken in by Mengele. As Leopold's son Richard Lowy later said, the pair were torn apart from the rest of their family – their parents, grandparents, eldest sister and the sister's baby were murdered on arrival. Three other sisters were taken to a forced labour camp.

Meanwhile, another twin brother and sister were brought to the camp. Kalman Bar-on and his sister were 13 when they arrived, and they joined the Lowy twins, two years older, in the twins' barracks. Kalman was deeply religious. He had been transported to Nazi-occupied Poland from a Hungarian yeshiva, or religious seminary. He was confused and frightened.

The four children, being twins, had been selected to live, and to undergo medical experimentation by Mengele. Those in the twins camp did what they could to support and help each other, but it was outside the barracks that Leopold and Kalman became friends.

The two boys were recruited as servants in the guard barracks, which meant they became eyewitnesses to much of what was happening in the camp. They were placed in the guard post to serve the troops. They were able to look over the guards' shoulders and see everything going on from that vantage point – the selections, the Roma camp, the transports, the uprisings.

They were also within 140 metres (150 yards) of the gas chambers, from which they could hear screaming.

Leopold, whom Richard later described as streetwise, took it upon himself to protect the young religious student – they looked out for each other, stole food for each other. Leopold said Kalman was a naïve, religious boy. He was dangerously unaware of the brutal reality they faced. His innocence threatened to draw the attention of the SS guards.

In his testimony, Kalman described their bond – calling Leopold "Lippa", he said that every morning at 5.15 a.m. they began their day of work. Lippa was his best friend, who saved him from many beatings, and he had been looking everywhere for him for 56 years.

When the camp was liberated in 1945, the twins went their separate ways, not even knowing each other's full names.

Lippa was in the US, not talking about Auschwitz. Richard Lowy, who has written about his father's friendship with Kalman in the 2025 book *Kalman & Leopold: Surviving*

THE TWINS

Mengele's Auschwitz, said it was not until the death of his aunt in 1999 that he started to find out about his father's time in Auschwitz – Leopold had never spoken about it. He managed to get his father to travel to Poland to visit his former home in Berehove, to look at the cattle cars on which the Jews were transported and, finally, to visit the remains of Auschwitz-Birkenau. Richard made a documentary, *Leo's Journey*, based on the visit. It was shown on Israeli television and seen by Kalman Bar-on – who recognized his friend Lippa straight away.

A few months later, Richard reunited the two. As he told *The Jewish Independent*, their reunion in their 70s was a moment beyond words. In that instant, they were no longer old men. They were boys again, transported back in time to when their survival depended on each other.

Although Leopold died shortly after their meeting in 2002, Kalman remained a valuable source of information about what they had gone through and the conditions at the camp, which his parents and siblings had not survived.

Both Kalman and Leopold had survived Auschwitz, survived Mengele and outlived their tormentors and would-be assassins, and they had brought up families of their own. Their experiment – how to live and bear witness – goes on, long after those of Mengele have stopped, and is in its own way a memorial to all the twins who lived, died and survived Auschwitz.

A BROTHER'S LOVE

It was the spring of 1944, just a few weeks before the D-Day landings which would all but seal the outcome of the war, the seaborne invasion of Western Europe by Allied troops that would liberate France and eventually lead to the end of Nazi Germany. For Hitler and his henchmen, including those in charge of the concentration camps, it was the beginning of the end, and what was once a ruthless killing machine started to splutter and grind to a halt. Chaos began to replace order.

As the Allies approached, Germany stepped up its campaign for the Final Solution in the east, and Hungarian Jews became the main target. Hungarian towns and villages were swept for Jews, and those who were caught were immediately put on trains to Dachau, to Bergen-Belsen – and to Auschwitz. One 12-year-old, Yitzchak Perlmutter – later called Ivor Perl – was captured with the rest of his family in the Hungarian town of Makó.

Born on 4 February 1932, he had already experienced a great deal of anti-Semitism in his short life. He told the Holocaust Memorial Day Trust that on the streets, he had stones thrown at him, abuse shouted at him and his hat knocked off his head on multiple occasions.

STORIES OF HOPE FROM AUSCHWITZ

In March 1944, the Hungarian fascist party, the Arrow Cross Party, gained power and levels of anti-Semitism increased. For the first time, Hungarian Jews were forced to wear the yellow star, and they were no longer allowed to have contact with non-Jews. And then the raids came.

At first the 12-year-old Yitzchak was, he admitted later, excited – he had rarely been on a train before. He and the other villagers also had no real idea of what Auschwitz was. But the train, far from being a treat, was hell – there was no access to water or food, and of course no sanitation. As was the case with all of the cattle cars, victims had to go to the toilet where they stood. The dehumanization process had begun.

When they got off the train, Yitzchak pretended to be 16, as he had been told, and was sent to the right-hand queue. His mother, younger sister and little brother went left – to the gas chambers. Terrified of being separated from his mother, the young boy tried to switch queues. But his mother made him go and stand with his brother Alec. He never saw her again.

After being stripped, examined and placed in the prison garb, it was time for him to receive his tattoo. But so large was the intake that day that the queue was too long to get everyone done. Yitzchak was sent to the barracks and brought back the next day. But now the ink had run out. He was told his number was 112021 – he has never forgotten it – but it was never tattooed on his arm.

Talking to *The Guardian* nearly 80 years after liberation, Yitzchak had an astonishing confession to make. A decade after he had left Auschwitz and emigrated to Britain, he considered having the tattoo done himself. Without a tattoo, he felt as if he wasn't "a fully-fledged survivor". This is another form of survivor's guilt.

As with every survivor, there were many moments when the tissue between life and death was very thin indeed. He recalled a time when an air raid siren rang out. Everyone, guards and inmates, ran for cover. Yitzchak ran back to the children's barracks, but his brother Alec told him to leave the barracks and take cover with him. He resisted, because he was afraid he would get in trouble – which may have meant death – but eventually relented and went with Alec.

They spent the night in hiding, terrified of being caught, and in the morning both melted back into the crowd as best they could. Yitzchak edged his way back to the children's block and snuck inside. It was empty. That morning every other child in his block had been taken to the gas chamber.

Yitzchak, like so many survivors, had no sympathy for the idea that there was anything special about them or their behaviour which meant they survived. It was simply luck, he later said.

He also spoke about the other potential killer – hunger. As he told *The Guardian*, starvation had changed him into someone he would later be ashamed of. If the person next to you died, you took their food and their shoes and were happy to do so. Another source of shame.

Gradually, as the war turned more and more in the Allies' favour, a sense of futility fell on the camp, especially among the guards. Hard labour schemes dried up, with just the occasional sudden recruitment of slaves for a factory. Yitzchak and Alec spent much of their time wandering around, or trying to find food scraps. Other inmates taught them places to hide so they could rest if and when they were given any work to do.

But conditions were still brutal, and the brutality was inflicted by other human beings. The brothers were arguing one day when one of the kapos – prisoners chosen from among the Jewish inmates to run the barracks – ordered them to fight properly. They fought, Yitzchak said, with tears running down their faces from the shame and pain, hitting each other until the kapo was satisfied.

In January 1945 the camp was about to be liberated, and the Nazis started destroying evidence, which also meant destroying the gas chambers and trying to get everyone who was left offsite. Yitzchak and Alec found themselves on a train to Kaufering concentration camp in Germany. If anything, it was worse there at this time than at Auschwitz – order had broken down entirely and almost no food or water was being supplied. Yitzchak remembered wheelbarrows being used to collect the dead and having to spend his days digging underground bases to hide military equipment – without tools.

Typhus swept through the camp often, and Yitzchak caught it. He was sent to the infirmary and, with almost non-existent medical care, he would have died, except Alec took it upon himself to go and get him, carrying him out over his shoulders.

After the brothers had spent a few months at Kaufering, the Nazis moved the prisoners on again, marching them for seven days to Dachau in the spring of 1945. They arrived to find the camp, one of the last still operational,

A BROTHER'S LOVE

so overcrowded the inmates could barely move. The Nazi commanders were killing inmates as quickly as they could but could not keep up. As the Americans approached, an order was given to march a large number of those still interned, Yitzchak and Alec included, up a nearby hill and shoot them. But the order was ignored – those told to do it were frightened of the consequences for them once they had been captured, as they knew they soon would be.

A number of inmates escaped from the camp – security had now largely broken down – and took refuge in the forest. Yitzchak and Alec were among them. Finally, on 29 April 1945, US troops entered the camp, bringing with them the Red Cross, and the escapees returned. Shortly after, it was confirmed to Yitzchak and Alec that their parents and siblings were all dead.

In November 1945 they managed to get on a transport to England, where they both settled in London. When he was 18, Yitzchak met his future wife Rhoda and they married in 1953, going on to have four children, six grandchildren and four great-grandchildren.

For a long time Yitzchak would not talk about the Holocaust, except with his brother – even Rhoda knew little of what he had been through. Then in 1995 his synagogue invited a guest speaker to talk about Auschwitz. The speaker dropped out – and Yitzchak was asked to step in. Since then he has dedicated much of his life to sharing his testimony and bearing witness, to try and help prevent something like the Holocaust happening again.

He admits that sometimes he is not sure it is working – he looks at the world and thinks to himself, how much has all this talking helped?

But he still draws on one resource to keep going, a resource he first called on all those years ago in the camps. "Hope, you had to have. I'm convinced that all of us, without hope, wouldn't have lasted a day."

A NEW CALLING

It is no ordinary thing to make a major career change at the age of 70, but Renée Feller is no ordinary person, and this was no ordinary career change.

Born in Czechoslovakia in 1931, she had already experienced some trauma in her childhood – it can be easy to forget that those who went through the horrors of Auschwitz were not blank slates but could have already faced difficulties of their own. Feller's mother had died when she was six, and her father had married her cousin, who therefore became her stepmother.

She was sent with her family to Auschwitz in 1944. She would later say that she could remember before the train and after the train, but she could remember nothing about the actual journey – she believes it was so horrifying she has completely blocked it out. What she does remember is seeing her grandmother, an old woman, lifted up by two Gestapo officers and carried onto the train. She never saw her grandmother again.

Like so many others, she was advised to lie about her age when she arrived and told everyone she was 18. Her brother, a year and a half younger than her, could not pull off a similar trick. As Renée tells it, he was quite frail-looking even for his age, and when he was sent to the right-hand queue, she knew instinctively it would take him to a bad place.

As with all other new inductees she had her head shaved – and for a 13-year-old girl this was especially mortifying. Her solution was to take her underwear off and make a hat of it, so she felt less self-conscious.

In the barracks the inmates were given bunk beds – but not as we would know them. There were three levels, no pillows, no blankets – and each level was for at least ten people. They crowded in together, relying on each other for warmth. They were always woken at 4 a.m., for a roll call of every person in the barracks in case anyone had escaped – which no one ever did. Being counted, she would later say, was one of her main memories.

She survived her time at Auschwitz, she said, by trying not to be noticed – it was one of her survival mechanisms. She pretended to see nothing and pretended to hear nothing, she closed herself off from what was happening. This would not always work for everyone, but somehow she managed it. But it did have an effect on her afterwards – it would take many years of therapy for her to be able to open up about her experiences.

Later she was transferred to a work camp, and she was liberated in 1945. But that was not the end of the challenges that life was to throw at her. Sent to the US after the war, she carried the emotional scars of war but made a life there. This included three marriages and widowhood, during which she raised three daughters.

A NEW CALLING

She didn't tell her children about what she went through until many, many years later, because she thought she was doing them a favour by keeping it hidden, that it was better if they didn't know. She later said she didn't realize that it was important to talk about what she had experienced.

And then, at the age of 70, her life went in a completely new direction – she was ordained as a rabbi. It was, she said, an unconscious thing at first. She didn't know why she wanted to become a rabbi. But later on she realized it was because she wanted to be out there, to not hide anymore.

Becoming a rabbi meant that the little girl who had hidden herself away to keep herself alive, and who had spent her life trying to re-emerge, now had a public role in bringing people together and bearing witness not only to her own traumas, but to other people's joys. She said that through the decades it became easier to speak about it, "but it's still not easy. It's like a fantasy; very often it feels like a dream."

A LUCKY CHILD

That was the name of his biography – *A Lucky Child*. After suffering persecution by the Nazis for the first 11 years of life, how was it that Thomas Buergenthal could ever describe himself as lucky? In part it was because he survived. But it was also about what his experience in the camps compelled him to do afterwards.

He was born in May 1934 in the town of Ľubochňa, Czechoslovakia. His parents, Mundek and Gerda, were Jews who had fled the Nazi rise to power in Germany. They ran a hotel where they would house others who had fled. But by 1938 it was clear that the Nazis would soon take power, and the family escaped to Poland, in the hope that they would be able to go from there to England – but they were unable to do so. They moved with a number of other Jewish refugees to the Polish city of Kielce.

There they were part of a ghetto, kept captive by the Nazis, with the threat of death ever-present. In August 1942, Thomas and his parents survived the liquidation of the ghetto, during which German authorities sent 20,000 Jews to the Treblinka concentration camp to be killed. Instead, they were sent to a forced labour camp nearby. But it was a temporary reprieve. In August 1944 they were sent to Auschwitz.

As a ten-year-old, Thomas could not work – and on most days, a child his age would have been sent directly to the gas chamber on arrival. But for some reason – maybe something as simple as an administrative error – the day he arrived there was no selection process, and so he was sent with his father to the men's section of the camp, while his mother was sent to the women's.

Thomas and his father initially remained together in the men's camp, but shortly after arrival they were separated. It was the last time Thomas would see his father. He spent the next year in the camp carrying out the same labour as the adults, cold and hungry.

Then in January 1945 came the death march. Auschwitz closed down, and Thomas was sent with thousands of others on the long march to who knows where. He would later recall that anyone who stopped for too long from exhaustion was shot.

He had no idea if his parents were alive or dead. It was not until after the war that he discovered that his father had been transferred to Buchenwald and killed. At the end of the march, Thomas was sent by rail to the Sachsenhausen concentration camp, where he was liberated in April 1945.

Tommy was cared for by Polish soldiers and later placed in a Polish orphanage. The orphanage arranged for him to be sent to what was then Palestine. Miraculously, his mother, who had survived the camps, was able to find her son through Jewish agencies. Instead of being sent to Palestine he was reunited with her in her hometown, Göttingen,

A LUCKY CHILD

Germany, in December 1946. The 12-year-old Thomas had already lived a number of lifetimes. But the "lucky child" wanted to make sure that the victory of hope against the Nazis was complete.

In late 1951, when he was 17, his mother sent him to join his aunt, uncle and cousin in New Jersey. He was very intelligent and was offered a scholarship to Bethany College in West Virginia. While there he was given US citizenship and also offered a Rhodes Scholarship to move to the UK. Instead he stayed in the US and earned a law degree from New York University in 1960. He then earned a doctorate and a Master of Law degree from Harvard Law School.

It was then that Thomas decided to use his academic skills to ensure that the horrors perpetrated by the Nazis never happened again. He became a human rights lawyer and would later become a judge at the International Court of Justice, dealing with international law. In his memoir he would say that his Holocaust experience had a very substantial impact on the human being he became. He wanted to fight for justice. He had, he said, an obligation to both the dead and the survivors of Auschwitz.

He would go on to write some of the foundational texts on international law, while serving on committees such as the United Nations Truth Commission for El Salvador and various human rights delegations. He was also vice chairman of the Claims Resolution Tribunal for Dormant Accounts, which returned funds to Holocaust victims from bank accounts that had been seized by the Nazis, right up until his death in 2023, aged 89.

In 2016, Thomas received the Grand Cross of the Order of Merit, the German Federal Republic's highest tribute to an individual. He regarded it as Germany's apology to him for what had happened – and he accepted it in the spirit of reconciliation. He said that he had mellowed towards the Germans since the war – abstract hate had been transformed by his encounters with actual human beings.

But until the end he never forgot how easily civilization can turn to barbarism. He worried that the hope that had sustained his journey was being forgotten the further the world moved from the Holocaust. "The grass grows again, and the flowers grow. Who cares whatever happened on that ground?" he said. His job was to keep making sure they cared.

He died on 29 May 2023. He is survived by his wife, three sons, two stepchildren and ten grandchildren, of which two are lawyers – still fighting for justice for the individual and hope for humanity.

THERE IS A BIG HOUSE IN AUSCHWITZ

As we have seen, life in Auschwitz was, for Roma and Sinti inmates – as for everyone else – almost unbearable. Housed in intolerable, unsanitary conditions where disease was rampant, subject to acts of violence by the guards, made to work until they died and often sent to the gas chambers on the whims of the camp commanders, those interned there saw very few rays of hope.

After the working day, the roll call often went on well into the night, leaving nothing but the chance of a few hours' sleep before the horror started again. But some days the roll call was shorter, and on those days the inmates were able to enjoy a few hours of "free time" during which they would find what pleasures they could as a community. During this small amount of free time, the prisoners gathered around the barracks, where they talked to each other, sold or exchanged things or visited each other in their respective barracks. Families, separated during the day, would come back together and share their meagre rations.

It was also a time of music.

STORIES OF HOPE FROM AUSCHWITZ

Romani and Sinti music is a hugely important part of their culture. As a traditionally nomadic people, songs have long been part of the glue that has held communities together, both as they moved through space and as they moved through time. It is a keeper of folk memory, and songs have mutated over the centuries as they have been passed down through generations, from singer to singer, from community to community.

Being nomadic, the Romani people often incorporated musical traditions from the countries where they lived into their own music, such as instruments, languages and the subject matter of the songs. This also helps create a musical landscape that tells the story of their travels.

The songs are generally of two distinct types. The first is fast music, music to dance to. The fast melodies are accompanied by the audience with hand-clapping, the clicking of wooden spoons, tongue-clicking and other percussive techniques. It is party music, to be sung at celebrations, at the coming together of people, in the middle of the night after a few drinks.

The second type of song is slow and plaintive. These are storytelling songs, about love, love lost, tragedy and sorrow. Like American blues music or Greek rebetiko, the songs are made to be cathartic – by sharing in the singer's sadness, we are made to feel cleansed of our own.

At the "Gypsy Camp" at Auschwitz, where there was little cause for celebration, and little strength left for dancing, there is no need to guess which sort of music was predominant.

THERE IS A BIG HOUSE IN AUSCHWITZ

In the free time that prisoners sometimes had, many of the traditional Romani songs were sung, providing a link to the past and to the outside world. By singing the songs that had been passed down by parents, grandparents and beyond, the inmates were able to remember a time before the camps and dream of a time after it, when their own children would pass down the tradition.

And, with so many different communities gathered together, they were able to exchange songs, compare the versions sung by their own community to those of another, and create new pieces, incorporating different traditions. This became part of the way in which Romani from diverse places came together as a community.

But as well as the traditional songs, the musicians also created new songs, sometimes based on traditional melodies, which told of what they were going through at that moment. This was the music of the camps, the music of Auschwitz, whose lyrics in Romani describe the miserable life they were experiencing – such as *"Labesbryku, éj, Osvěnčinatar amen dine"*: "From Auschwitz we were taken to Ravensbrück".

Others included *"Andr'oda taboris"* ("In the Camp"), while the traditional Romani love song *"Čhajori romaňi"* ("Little Roma Girl"), apparently had a verse added by Slovak Roma during World War Two that reflects the painful experiences of that time.

But the most famous and enduring of these is the song *"Aušvicate hi kher baro"*, generally translated as "There is a Big House in Auschwitz". Believed to use the melody of a traditional song of one of the Romani communities, *"Oda kalo čirikloro"* ("The Black Bird"), it has come to symbolize the plight of the Roma and Sinti people in Auschwitz and the other concentration camps. The lyrics describe the inhumane conditions in Auschwitz: hunger, hard work, violence, and mass murder in the gas chambers.

As with most Romani songs, the lyrics are not fixed, and the number of verses differs depending on the version. As with most folk music, oral transmission affects what is sung. Variants of the song were recorded after the war in Poland, Moravia and Slovakia, and then in many other places.

One famous version was sung by Margita Nova, born in a Romani settlement near Liptovský Mikuláš, Czechoslovakia, in 1935. Her mother and father both died in the war, her father killed by wartime violence, her mother dying after going into labour prematurely and not being able to access medical help. Margita was one of eight children left after their deaths. Her mother's dying wish that the children not be separated was impossible to honour, and they were placed apart.

Margita was adopted at age 12 by Jozef and Anna Holomek – they had changed their obviously Romani name of Hranek at the start of the war – joining their 11 children, and becoming particularly close to one of the girls, called Barka. Margita could not read and didn't attend school, but she worked around the house – and began to sing.

It was here that she learnt *"Aušvicate hi kher baro"*, which she would then perform throughout her life. When she and Barka were adults, in the 1960s, they went to visit the "big house in Auschwitz", and Margita reported being especially moved by the children's shoes on display in the museum – every one the shoe of a child who had been gassed.

THERE IS A BIG HOUSE IN AUSCHWITZ

But perhaps the most famous version of *"Aušvicate hi kher baro"* was performed after the war by Růžena Danielová from South Moravia, herself a survivor of Auschwitz.

Růžena Danielová was born on 27 February 1904 in Čejč, Hodonín district, Czechoslovakia. Her mother was blind, but was a powerful singer, and she taught her daughter to sing. From the age of 16, Růžena lived with Martin Daniel as they moved around Czechoslovakia and neighbouring countries. In the years 1920 to 1927, they settled in the village of Kobylí (Břeclav district), and got married in 1926.

The marriage produced six children, sons František, Jan, Tomáš, Michal and daughters Magdalena and Zuzana. Růžena, Martin and the five surviving children moved in 1927 to the Romani colony in Břeclav, and then in 1938 to Mutěnice, where they built a small house. Růžena, her husband and the eldest son Jan worked in various brickyards. They also helped with seasonal work in the vineyards and during the harvest. It was a traditional Romani life.

In 1943, the Nazi German government started rounding up everyone they categorized as "racially gypsy". As the *Encyclopaedia of the Nazi Genocide of the Sinti and Roma in Europe* notes, on the advice of local residents, Růžena and Martin tried to save themselves and their family by marrying their pregnant daughter Magdalena to her non-Roma boyfriend (who was from Velvary in Central Bohemia). Needless to say, it did not work. On 7 May 1943, they were all taken to Auschwitz-Birkenau.

Růžena would be the only survivor in her family – her husband and all of her children were killed between August and December 1943. In the "Gypsy Camp" there was never any mystery as to where someone's family had gone, as there was in other parts of the camp – they were no longer there, and so they were dead. And Růžena would have had to listen to the roll call announcing their deaths on the day they died.

She herself was the victim of medical experimentation – at one stage she received an injection into her skull, having no idea what it was. She continued to suffer from violent headaches for the rest of her life.

On 2 August 1944, just before the liquidation of the camp, Růžena was transferred to the Ravensbrück concentration camp – still fit for work, she was not selected for the gas chamber. Assigned to work in a factory in Wittenberg, she was liberated there in 1945.

Until her death on 3 May 1988, she lived in the village of Hrubá Vrbka in what is now the Czech Republic, and was known for her singing of *"Aušvicate hi kher baro"*. She lived with her partner, the musician Pavel Kubík. He had survived the war with the help of local people and, in a cruel irony, a local fascist organization which spared a few musicians in that area, including the violinist Jožka Kubík, who would later find some international fame.

Růžena Danielová's story was transcribed in the 1970s by ethnomusicologist Dušan Holý, who published it in 1993, and she would feature heavily in the 1997 film documentary *Ó, ty černý ptáčku* (*Oh, You Black Bird: The Forgotten Holocaust of the Romanies*) by director Břetislav Rychlík.

But it was in the world-acclaimed documentary *Latcho Drom*, by the French director Tony Gatlif that the song, sung by Margita Makulová, achieved international recognition, symbolizing in the film both the tragedy and the resilience of the Roma and Sinti people.

A song like *"Aušvicate hi kher baro"* illuminates the strength and hope of a community which still exists, many, many years after Nazi Germany has been consigned to the trash can of history.

THE PORTRAITS

She could, she always said, still draw their faces exactly from memory. When Halina Ołomucka was asked by SS guards to draw or paint their portraits, she would look deep into their eyes, study their faces and make a creative record as much in her mind as on the paper. To the guards she was performing a service. To herself she was bearing witness, and she would continue to do so for the rest of her life.

Ołomucka was born in Warsaw on 24 November 1921. Her father Andrzej was a newspaper salesman who died when she was five; her mother was called Hadassah. She had one brother. Right from the start she showed great artistic talent and was seemingly never without a pencil or a paintbrush in her hand, capturing the world around her. And that world was to take a very dark turn.

When the Nazis invaded in 1939, 17-year-old Ołomucka, her mother and brother were sent to the Warsaw ghetto. The largest of Nazi Germany's ghettos, at its height it was believed to hold 460,000 Jews, all kept prisoner on subsistence rations before being sent off to the death camps. Ołomucka was assigned to a labour battalion operating outside the ghetto walls, which she would go out to every day and work. This allowed her to smuggle some food back into the ghetto – at the risk of her life – to share with those around her.

She also managed to smuggle in some artist's materials, paper and pencils, and to start to record images of the ghetto. Again, had she been caught, the punishment may have been death – but for Halina Ołomucka drawing was like breathing, she could not stop.

In May 1943, she and her mother were herded to the Umschlagplatz, the holding area beside the train station, and then placed on a train and transported to the Majdanek concentration camp, while her brother was sent elsewhere. At the camp, her mother was immediately selected for death and sent to the gas chamber, while Ołomucka was spared – she was deemed fit enough for work. The work was back-breaking and shredded her fingers – but still she drew whenever she could, on whatever she could. It was forbidden, but it was necessary – a part of her that the Nazis could not take away.

Gradually the work began to grind her down, and one day she found she could not get out of bed – she remembered lying in bed waiting for death. But then came a moment that changed everything, and it was the start of her fight back against those who sought to kill her.

The block leader came into the barracks and asked if anyone could draw. She volunteered and was made to show her talents – if the block leader was unimpressed she would have died or been killed. She passed the test and was assigned to paint propaganda slogans on the barrack walls, for which she received extra rations. These she shared, but

THE PORTRAITS

she also used them to regain the strength that had almost completely left her body, nearly killing her.

Her food ration went up again when she was asked by the camp administration to draw pictures of the camp itself, particularly of the guards. These too would be used for propaganda, showing the camp in the best light. She was given a room in which to do these drawings and paintings, although she still had to do her manual work.

Unbeknown to the Nazis, she would also smuggle some of the art supplies back to her barracks, where she would paint her fellow inmates. These pictures were hidden away and smuggled out of the camp.

From Majdanek, Ołomucka was transported to Auschwitz, where she received the number 48652. She worked in a factory, but again she was asked to paint and draw the Germans – the guards at Auschwitz were especially interested in portraits of themselves. It was here that Ołomucka stared into the eyes of evil, and each face, she said, was burned into her mind, so that even years later she could still see them, and draw them, perfectly.

Again she smuggled equipment out, and again she took it upon herself to draw her fellow inmates. These faces too stayed with her. For those she drew it was a deeply poignant moment – they believed, and were mostly correct, that these portraits would be the only record of them that survived the war.

Her painting kept her alive as a person, and it also kept her alive in practice, as the popularity of her work saved her from the gas chamber. On 18 January 1945, she was part of a group that set off from Auschwitz on a death march to the Ravensbrück camp, and from there to Neustadt-Glewe. Many died on the march; she managed to survive.

After the war ended, she returned to Warsaw. She was informed that her brother and relatives had also perished. She moved to Łódź and was accepted into the Academy of Fine Arts, studying under the famous painter Władysław Strzemiński. Now she could paint other topics, and she sometimes did – but her work kept returning to the horrors of the Holocaust. As she repeatedly stated, she felt compelled to perpetuate the memory of the concentration camp victims. She also strove to warn the world about the horrors of war so that it would never happen again.

Her work is one of the great testaments to the victims of the Holocaust. It is also one of the great testaments of hope. In Auschwitz, the Nazis tried to kill not only the human, but the human spirit. Halina Ołomucka is proof that there are some parts of the human soul that they could not touch, let alone destroy.

WE ARE FREE

The morning before, like every morning, the inmates at Auschwitz had been standing at attention for roll call before being assigned work. Today, however, a camp guard asked if anyone spoke German.

Gene Klein raised his hand. As he later said, he did not know what was going to happen, but nothing could be worse than the suffering he was undergoing anyway. Still a teenager, born in Czechoslovakia, hungry and suffering, he thought at that moment that if he was taken out and shot, it would be better than living.

But instead he was given to an SS sergeant, who took him outside the gates. He was, the sergeant said, a civil engineer, and for the next few weeks he would be doing a survey for a new road. Klein was there, he told him, to help him with his equipment, and they spent the day doing the initial work.

The next day, Klein and the engineer worked until just after lunch time. Then the engineer said to Klein, "I see what terrible situation you people are in." He took him to the outside of the army barracks beside the camp. He would stay outside, he told Klein, and the inmate should go in and feel under the first table.

Gene Klein did so. There he found, wrapped in a napkin and attached to the underside of the table, a piece of real bread such as he hadn't seen for months, a piece of cheese, and a cup of milk. He drank the milk, as it could not be transported, but the food he kept and shared among his fellow inmates. The German engineer did this each day, and it was never discussed.

Gene Klein survived Auschwitz and for three decades remained silent about his time there. But eventually he decided the world needed to keep being reminded of the terrible legacy of Auschwitz and the Holocaust.

In the spring of 1944, 16-year-old Klein and his family were taken from their village in Hungary and thrown into Auschwitz. Before that, his was a middle-class Hungarian family living in a small town in the foothills of the Carpathian Mountains. He would later remember sitting in outdoor cafes on summer evenings and skating on the river on winter afternoons. His father owned a hardware store, was an avid soccer fan and loved to tend to his garden. His mother took care of him and his two sisters. She was always preoccupied with getting him to eat more. They were not wealthy, but had everything they needed.

But in 1944 that all changed – he father's store was confiscated, he was thrown out of school, and the family was forced to wear the yellow star. Then they were rounded up and put aboard a cattle car to Auschwitz.

On arrival, his father was taken straight to the gas chamber. Klein would later say that a man in a black uniform sent him in one direction and his father in another. "Then

WE ARE FREE

there is smoke coming out of a chimney and someone says: 'Your father is up there.'"

Klein was sent to do hard labour, spending months before and after his encounter with the engineer living through all the sufferings which the inmates of Auschwitz were subject to – the beatings, the starvation, having the person next in line collapse and die, and the stench of the smoke always billowing from the chimneys of its crematoria.

Somehow, Klein survived, and later he remembered in tears the day that the camp was liberated.

He had become friends with two Polish boys about his age; the three of them would often wake early and go outside. It was the only time they could find some peace. Once everyone else woke, he said, the screaming and the crying would begin. It was also not uncommon to find that the person in the next camp bed who went to sleep the night before was dead by morning – getting up early avoided confronting this.

The camp, he said, apart from being brutal, was also monotonous, the same things day in, day out, so anything out of the ordinary was leapt upon and talked about. "Is this good news or bad news?" One morning, when the sky was thick with fog, the three boys came out early as usual and noticed something strange. There were no guards in the guard towers – this had never happened before, even for a moment. They decided to sneak across the camp and check out the gate – there were no guards there either. They dared each other to go up to the gate, which they found was still padlocked.

Then there was a break in the fog, like a mirage. They saw a horse with a horseman, coming closer. One of the Polish kids said to Klein, "Look at his hat" – it was a red star, a Russian soldier. The boys were stunned and confused. The man took out his gun, and shot off the padlock, telling the boys that food and medical help were on their way.

The three boys ran to every barrack in the vicinity, opened up the doors and in every language they knew, started yelling, "We are free! We are free!" Klein said that those who were able to walk out, walked out, and those who couldn't walk, crawled.

Klein himself decided to go and look at the SS bungalows on site. They were all empty. He broke into one and found a closet full of clothes and a pantry full of food. But even better, he went to the bathroom and turned on a tap. For the first time since he had arrived he felt hot water. There were fluffy towels. Shampoo. Soap. It was at that moment, he said, that he "gave a little victory dance". He took off his prisoner uniform and had his first hot shower in a year.

For months afterwards, he would still wake in the night and think he was back in the camp. But then he would remind himself, "We are free! We are free!"

Gene Klein emigrated to the US after the war and has become an advocate not only for those who died in, and those who survived, the concentration camps, but for the vigilance that it requires to stop any repeat. He told Fort Hays State University in 2017, that he would continue to tell his story to show the tolerance and compassion necessary to prevent what happened to them happening to others.

WE ARE FREE

We must all watch for this around us but also inside ourselves. If we do so, we can stop the next Auschwitz. This is Gene Klein's message of hope.

IF THIS IS A MAN

When Primo Levi was taken to Auschwitz he was a simple chemistry student. By the time he left he was a spokesperson for every man, woman and child who had lived in, died in or survived the camps. In his books, *If This Is a Man*, *The Truce*, *The Sixth Day*, *The Periodic Table* and *The Wrench*, he provided a chronicle of the suffering endured by the inmates of Auschwitz, but also stories of hope, of camaraderie and resilience. The mere act of writing them is a testament to these three virtues.

Levi was born in Turin, Italy, on 31 July 1919. His father Cesare was in manufacturing, his mother Rina was well educated, an avid reader who played the piano and spoke fluent French. He had one younger sister, Anna Maria, whom he would stay close to all his life.

While he was also a reader, his true interest lay in science. As a young adult, he would have been astonished to know that he eventually became a writer. He was a brilliant student, and at age 11 he was fast-tracked to high school. He was the only Jew, and for the first time he was subject to anti-Semitism. He later wrote that only two boys had taunted him, but it remained a major trauma – having always been celebrated for his intellect, he was now being mocked for his "race".

In July 1934, at the age of 15, he sat the exams for the Liceo Classico Massimo D'Azeglio school, specializing in the classics, and was admitted that year. Here he was one of six Jews, but the taunting continued and grew greater. The world was slipping towards war, and Italy's Fascist government under Benito Mussolini, in power since 1922, was becoming ever more closely aligned to Nazi Germany, with its anti-Semitic laws.

Levi had decided he wanted to be a chemist and enrolled at the University of Turin in 1937. At that time Jews were allowed to study at university, but the enactment of the Italian Racial Laws of October 1938 stopped anyone Jewish from studying and publishing. Jewish students who had begun their course of study, including Levi, were permitted to continue, but new Jewish students were barred from entering university. Levi found it nearly impossible to find someone to supervise his thesis, especially after Italy's war began in June 1940.

With Jews now losing virtually all access to jobs and homes, Levi joined the Italian Resistance in October 1943 and saw action in the hills around the Alps. But on 13 December 1943 he and his comrades were captured. Believing he was about to be executed as an antifascist, he decided to tell his captors he was a Jew, which changed his status. Instead of being shot, he was sent to the prison camp at Fossoli, and then on to Auschwitz. Throughout his life Levi battled with whether he had made the right decision.

IF THIS IS A MAN

Fossoli was no preparation for Auschwitz. As Levi later said, the conditions in the camp were quite good, with no talk of executions. The atmosphere was quite calm. They worked in the kitchen in turn and performed other services in the camp. They even prepared a dining room.

At the time the camp was in Italian hands, but it was soon taken over by the Germans. They started arranging the deportation of inmates to the death camps, and on 21 February 1944, Levi and other inmates were transported in 12 cramped cattle trucks to Buna/Monowitz, one of the three main camps in the Auschwitz complex. Levi became prisoner number 174517. It was to be the start of 11 months of hell on earth.

Levi arrived at Auschwitz at what was perhaps the height of its powers as a killing machine. The average life expectancy of a new entrant to the camp at that time was three to four months – those who weren't gassed would be worked to death. Of the 650 Italian Jews in his transport, Levi, who was 23 when he arrived, was one of only 20 who left the camp alive.

Levi's main aim in the camp was to go unnoticed. He found a friend in Lorenzo Perrone. Perrone was not a prisoner at the camp but worked there as a mason on the building works. He was no Nazi sympathizer – he hated them and would often share the extra rations he received with the inmates at great risk to himself.

Each day he managed to get a bowl of soup for Levi – the pair liked each other and shared a language, Piemontese. The soup was worth, Levi thought, about 500 calories a day. He credited Perrone with his life and named both his children after him, Lisa Lorenza and Renzo Cesare, as well as securing him the Israeli honour as one of the Righteous among the Nations. Perrone also had letter-writing privileges and was able to send postcards to Levi's mother – his father had died of cancer in 1942 – letting her know in code that her son was still alive.

Levi would later write in *If This Is a Man* that Perrone was a very silent man who refused his thanks. He just shrugged and said, "Take the bread. Take the sugar. Keep silent, you don't need to speak."

But after the war Perrone would struggle with what he had seen at Auschwitz, turning to alcohol. He caught tuberculosis, and Levi arranged for him to be hospitalized. Perrone kept leaving the hospital to find alcohol. When Levi visited and tried to talk about Auschwitz, Perrone asked him to leave. He died on 30 April 1952 of tuberculosis. At his funeral Levi said that he believed it was really due to Lorenzo that he was alive.

As a chemist, Levi was able to secure work as an assistant in IG Farben's Buna Werke laboratory that was aiming to produce synthetic rubber. It saved him from hard labour, but for the sensitive and empathetic Levi, every privilege – from his work to the bowls of soup – was also a source of guilt.

For the next few months Levi watched as the brutality continued, but also as Auschwitz started to decline as the Allies came ever closer. Work dried up, and more and more time was spent with inmates just sitting around, and occasionally dropping dead from lack of food. The chimneys of the crematoria stopped producing smoke made from burning humans. The factory where he worked was closed.

IF THIS IS A MAN

Shortly before the camp was liberated by the Red Army, he fell ill with scarlet fever and was placed in the camp's infirmary. This would spare him going on the death march of 18 January 1945, another source of guilt.

The camp was finally liberated on 27 January 1945. Levi did not reach Turin until 19 October 1945. In his book *The Truce*, he would write that the long railway journey home to Turin took him on a circuitous route from Poland, to Belarus, Ukraine, Romania, Hungary, Austria and Germany.

Levi found work in a paint factory just outside Turin and seemed set to return to his life as a chemist. But in the long hours spent alone in the dormitory of the factory, he started to write down what had happened to him. It took him ten months. On 22 December 1946, the manuscript was complete. In the meantime he had met and fallen in love with Lucia Morpurgo, who helped him edit the manuscript. They married in September 1947 and the book was published a month later in a small print run of 2,000 copies. It seemed destined to disappear. But in 1959 it was translated into both English and German, and it became a sensation.

Levi would spend the rest of his life chronicling his experiences at Auschwitz, and especially his own complicated feelings then and after. He became one of Italy's premier writers, and *The Truce* has long been on school curriculums there, as it is throughout the world. His final book, *The Drowned and the Saved*, explored why people behaved as they did in Auschwitz, and also what it meant that some died and some were saved. It is an exploration of fate and fortune, of despair and hope.

STORIES OF HOPE FROM AUSCHWITZ

On 11 April 1987, Levi died after a fall from the interior landing of his third-storey apartment in Turin. Doubts remain as to whether it was suicide or an accident. Just before he died he had called his rabbi to tell him how difficult he was finding it looking into the face of his mother, who was dying of cancer. Her face reminded him of the faces of the suffering in Auschwitz. Fellow writer and Auschwitz survivor Elie Wiesel was in no doubt: "Primo Levi died at Auschwitz 40 years later."

Levi wrote thousands of words about his experiences of Auschwitz, but ultimately he felt that it was a few words of Lorenzo Perrone – a man of few words – that summed everything up. In *Moments of Reprieve*, Levi quoted Perrone: "He asked me once in very laconic words: Why are we in the world if not to help each other?"

SO WE DON'T GET LOST

She called her memoir *The Triumph of Hope*, and everything about Ruth Elias's story tells us that it was a triumph hard won.

She was born Ruth Huppert in 1922 in Moravská Ostrava, Czechoslovakia. Her parents divorced when she and her older sister were young, and the siblings lived for a time with their paternal grandfather, and then with an uncle and aunt.

When Germany invaded in 1939, they became subject to the anti-Semitic laws of the Third Reich, and Ruth was forced to leave school, and her uncle and aunt lost their house. She and her sister found work through her father's contacts on a farm in Brno. But in 1942, Ruth and her family were deported to Theresienstadt ghetto, where she married her boyfriend, Koni, a ghetto policeman. She and Koni built an apartment for themselves.

Ruth became pregnant. What should have been a joyful event, however, was a disaster. She begged the doctors in the ghetto to terminate the baby, but as abortion is generally forbidden in Jewish law, unless the life of the mother is at risk, they would not perform the procedure. Unlike many who followed, they did not know that the mother's life was now at risk in the worst way possible.

She and Koni were taken on a transport to the family camp of Auschwitz, where both were forced to undertake hard labour, which for Ruth meant moving rocks around, while trying to hide her condition. After briefly working in a leather workshop, she was transferred from the family camp to the women's camp – and was back to clearing rocks and rubble. She was now more advanced in her condition, and it soon became evident to the other women what was happening. Many tried to protect her, but one decided to report her.

This was at the start of Josef Mengele's phase of experimenting on children, and so the baby was allowed to come to full term. She did not give her daughter a name. Every name she could think of reminded her of someone in her family. Knowing her child's fate, she called her simply "my child".

And then Ruth was put through grotesque suffering – her breasts were tied so they could not produce milk. The doctors wanted to establish how long the baby daughter would survive without being fed. Ruth managed to get a few scraps of bread into her little girl, but it was a losing battle, and one of the prisoner doctors, possibly Gisella Perl, managed to obtain some morphine to end the horror by ending the girl's life.

Ruth was again moved, this time to Taucha, a subcamp of Buchenwald, where inmates were forced to produce rocket launchers, and where she worked as a translator.

While there she met the man who would bring her hope – Kurt Elias. They met while rehearsing for a cabaret the prisoners had been ordered to perform. They became inseparable, and when the camp was liberated in April 1945, they stayed behind to help tend the sick. They returned to Czechoslovakia, where Ruth divorced Koni, and Kurt found that his wife and son had perished. Ruth also found that all the other members of her family had died.

On 18 April 1947 they married. Kurt became a pharmacologist and Ruth began working for a Dutch shipping company. And then in 1949 the pair emigrated to Israel.

"There is no question that our place is in Israel," she told *The Jewish News* in 1999. "Despite the hard life, the fears, I am a very, very proud Israeli." She and Kurt had a family – children and then grandchildren. Initially when their children asked about the numbers tattooed on their parents' arms, Ruth and Kurt lied to them, telling them it was so they didn't get lost.

Auschwitz had made her, she said, appreciate every moment. "I am aware of the beauty of life," she said. "I've got a garden, my children nearby. A flower, a bird, music, people… I enjoy everything."

A triumph of hope.

FINAL WORD

Reading about Auschwitz can be harrowing – perhaps never in human history have the depths of human depravity been so exposed and so organized. The brutality was relentless and, at its worst, of an efficiency which remains hard to comprehend.

Moments of hope were fleeting and sometimes just led to greater despair. There are few heartwarming moments, no stories of puppy dogs found and adopted – Auschwitz is notorious for having no birds above it, back when it was running and even now. It is like nature itself knows that this is a place of evil.

And yet astonishingly, some light does shine through – moments of courage and humanity, whether it is sharing a piece of bread or making music or art. The Nazis attempted to dehumanize and then exterminate entire communities of people. They tried to treat them as subhuman. They tried to eliminate them from the face of the earth. They failed. And they have been consigned to the trash can of history. Adolf Hitler dreamed that his Third Reich would last for a thousand years. It lasted little more than a decade.

STORIES OF HOPE FROM AUSCHWITZ

Every story of every survivor of Auschwitz is a story of hope – and hope fulfilled. Many of those who came through said that without hope they would not have made it. Even in the depths of horror, they knew that this was not who humans are – neither them nor their captors. Many of them have continued to tell their stories – to bear witness, to give their testimony so we do not forget.

And also so we do not repeat the horrors of Auschwitz. Let us dare to hope it never happens again, and work to making that, too, a hope fulfilled.

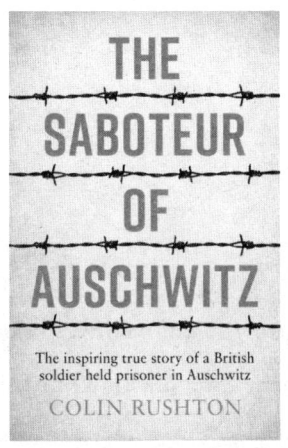

THE SABOTEUR OF AUSCHWITZ

The Inspiring True Story of a British Soldier
Held Prisoner in Auschwitz

Colin Rushton

Paperback
ISBN: 978-1-78783-329-6

In 1942, young British soldier Arthur Dodd was taken prisoner by the German Army and transported to Oswiecim in Polish Upper Silesia. The Germans gave it another name, now synonymous with mankind's darkest hours. They called it Auschwitz.

This shocking true story sheds new light on the operations at the camp, exposes a hierarchy of prisoner treatment by the SS and presents the largely unknown story of the military POWs held there.

Have you enjoyed this book?

If so, why not write a review on your favourite website?

If you're interested in finding out more about our books, find us on Facebook at **Summersdale Publishers** and on Instagram, TikTok and Bluesky at **@summersdalebooks** and get in touch. We'd love to hear from you!

Thanks very much for buying this Summersdale book.

www.summersdale.com